SUCCESSES
and
INDUSTRY FIRSTS

1940 - 1980

The memories live on ...
so does the pride.

by Paul Wallem

3 Point Ink, LLC

Successes and Industry Firsts
©2021 Paul Wallem
All Rights Reserved
ISBN 978-1-7923-6569-0

The IH logo, the IHC logo, and CaseIH, are trademarks of the International Truck & Engine Corporation and the Case New Holland Corporation. They are used for identification purposes only.

To contact the publisher:

> 3 Point Ink
> PO Box 519
> Greenville, IL 62246
> (618) 664-1550
> info@3pointink.com

Photo acknowledgments

Unless otherwise noted, all photos are courtesy of the Wisconsin Historical Society and/or Navistar International. Special thanks to Navistar Historian Tom Clark.

The painting featured on Page 51 was reproduced from a 1971 IH Farmall calendar. The artist was Thomas M. Hoyne.

Vintage signs are courtesy of Nelson Drummond at IHGear.com and Steve and Robin Reedy at Reedyvillegoods.com.

TABLE OF CONTENTS

Dedication	Joan Wallem	4
Introduction	Paul Wallem	5
Chapter One	IH During World War II	6
Chapter Two	Engine Design	23
Chapter Three	International Trucks	27
Chapter Four	Construction Equipment	33
Chapter Five	Tillage Tools	39
Chapter Six	Expansion	43
Chapter Seven	Axial-Flow Combine	49
Chapter Eight	2+2	63
Chapter Nine	Small Tractor Triumph	67
Chapter Ten	Replacing the Horse	75
Chapter Eleven	IH in the '50s	81
Chapter Twelve	World Headquarters	87
Chapter Thirteen	Combine Square Dances	97
Chapter Fourteen	A Personal First	103
Chapter Fifteen	Leaving the Iron Pusher Image Behind	115
Chapter Sixteen	The "International" of IH	124
Chapter Seventeen	Taking the Farm to the City	145
	Paquette Museum	148
Chapter Eighteen	Two Farm Boys and their Red Tractors	155
Chapter Nineteen	The IH Collectors Clubs	161
	Acknowledgments	169

Dedicated

To Joan, my wife of 65 years
and 17 moves

ABOUT THIS BOOK

During 1984, International Harvester reached a fork in the road. The farm equipment division went one way — with Case Corporation — while the motor truck division went a different direction and became Navistar.

Now, all these years later, red farm equipment with a new logo thrives. International trucks begin a larger worldwide presence as Navistar joins Traton.

You could call this book a sentimental journey through one of Harvester's most successful periods: 1940 to 1980. It was a time when the Company looked into the future and entered markets that had risk, but also great potential. It pursued the most promising and, despite Harvester's immense size, it was surprisingly nimble in its ability to design and engineer many industry-changing products.

The many IH successes were due, in large part, to the New Product Selection Committees. These committees, embedded in the engineering, manufacturing and marketing departments, met constantly to determine potential for new products.

It can be hard to properly judge the success of a product or program. Some fared better than others in different areas. For example, even though construction equipment didn't receive the attention of some other IH divisions, much of that equipment did quite well.

Included in this book are the most obvious successes and industry firsts, and some that may surprise you. Enjoy!

Paul Wallem

6   SUCCESSES AND FIRSTS

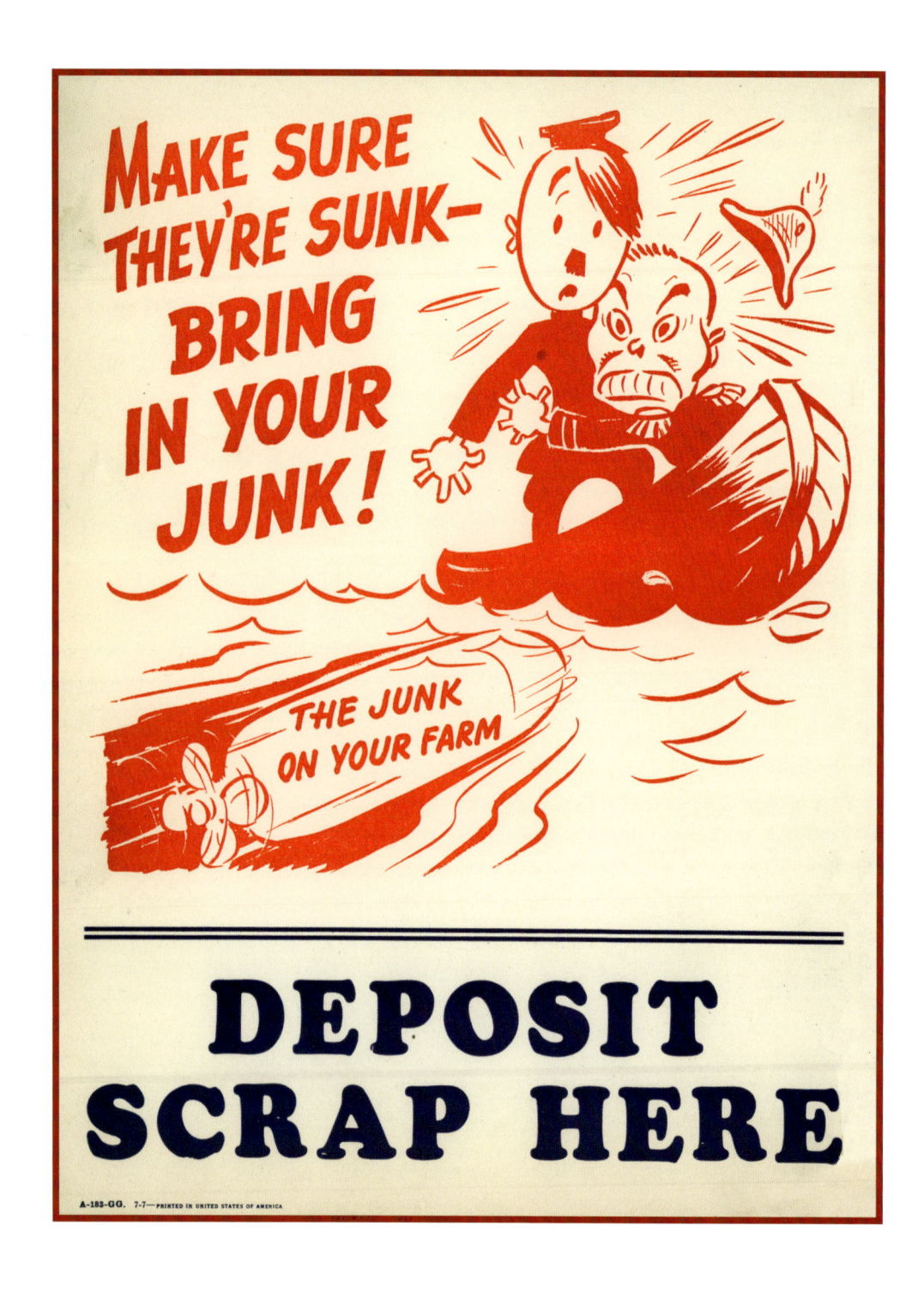

CHAPTER ONE

INTERNATIONAL HARVESTER DURING WORLD WAR II

This book starts at the beginning of World War II because many IH enthusiasts I've interviewed were unaware of the remarkable efforts of International Harvester during that period. When I joined the Company in 1955, virtually everyone in management positions were WWII veterans. Many had served with the Harvester Battalions, which I write about on page nine.

Immediately following the December 7, 1941 attack on Pearl Harbor, Harvester initiated three separate war efforts.

RUST HARVEST

The steel shortage had become a big problem. IH initiated a program called "Rust Harvest" by asking dealers to accumulate rusty farm equipment from customer

One of the collection yards for IH's "Rust Harvest"

fence rows. IH dealers nationwide responded in a big way, and Harvester recycled truckloads of old equipment into steel for war machines.

HARVESTER WAR PRODUCTION

A surprise during the research for this book was the extent to which Harvester built aerial torpedoes — torpedoes launched from a fixed-wing aircraft in flight. After hitting the water, the torpedo propelled itself to the target at a speed of about 33.5 knots with a range of up to 6,300 yards.

The Mark 13 torpedoes became a subject of pride at the factories when the U.S. Navy would award certificates for excellence of performance.

A telegram wired to the McCormick Works plant by Rear Admiral G. F. Hussey, Jr., Chief of Navy Ordnance in Washington, D.C., stated that IH-built torpedoes were instrumental in the sinking of several Japanese ships in the Pacific battle of Kyushu on April 7, 1945:

> *"... the mark 13 type aircraft torpedoes blew up and sank the mighty battleship Yamato, and a Gano class light cruiser, and several Tertusuki and Takanami class destroyers." "Harvester torpedoes were ready. That they accomplished their purpose effectively and surely is due to the diligence and skill which you have consistently applied to the manufacture of our torpedoes."*

Each torpedo had a serial number which the military tracked. The wire from Admiral Hussey listed the serial numbers of eight torpedoes built by Harvester that found their targets: 43507, 43788, 43791, 71489, 71565, 71568, 71574 and 72262.

The torpedoes were not built at one factory. The bodies were produced at the McCormick Works in Chicago, gyroscopes were made at the Milwaukee Works, and the screw machine parts at the West Pullman Works. Final assembly of the Mark 13 torpedoes was at the McCormick Works. Each weighed over 2,200 pounds.

As shown in the following graph, Harvester's wartime effort received 24 Excellence Awards for production of machines, armaments and ammunition.

> **Milwaukee Works** TORPEDOES, CANNON SHELLS, CRAWLERS
> **West Pullman Works** CANNON SHELLS
> **Wisconsin Steel Works** STEEL
> **Indianapolis Works** ANTI-AIRCRAFT GUN MOUNTS
> **St. Paul Works** ANTI-AIRCRAFT GUNS

International Harvester produced over $1 billion worth of war machines, materials and supplies during World War II. It was a huge response, and included a wide variety of products that aided the war effort, such as:

> Cargo trucks, bulldozers, tanks, blood bank refrigerators, power units, half-tracks, dump trucks, tractors, shells, gun mounts, high speed gun carriages, ambulances, mobile canteens, shells, firing pins, gun loaders, aircraft engine cowling assemblies, invasion ice chests, heavy duty trucks, tank transmissions, brake shoes, generators, gears, sprockets and countless other products.

On the next page are photos of a few of the military vehicles IH built.

Harvester's support of the military extended into the '50s. According to the U.S. Army Ordnance Corps, IH produced 337,623 M1 rifles from 1953 to 1956 at its Evansville plant, which had been building refrigeration equipment.

HARVESTER BATTALIONS

Not only was IH one of the largest manufacturers and suppliers of war goods to the military, over 21,100 of its employees served in uniform. In June, 1942, the U.S. Army requested that the Company form a Harvester Battalion to create a maintenance unit for the 12th Armored Division. One thousand employees immediately volunteered. In October 1942, a second battalion was formed for heavy tank maintenance. Four hundred-twenty-nine employees lost their lives in action.

SUCCESSES AND FIRSTS

The M-2-4 Troop Transport

The M-5 Half-track. Over 12,000 were built at the Springfield Works.

The M-5 Engineer Crawler

SUCCESSES AND FIRSTS   11

Invasion

In the high tide of invasion, east and west, thousands of International Diesel Tractors are serving the Army, the Navy, the Marine Corps, and the Air Forces. On many a battlefront they play a fighting part in the drama of tanks and ships and fighting men.

Take Guadalcanal. In the tense hours of that first invasion it was *do or die* on the airstrip. International Diesels went ashore with their bulldozers . . . filled in craters as fast as enemy bombs dug them . . . did combat duty to help the Marines cling to the toehold that gave us Henderson Field. Many a tractor operator died there, under fire, but the great Pacific Offensive was on.

It is the year of decision—overseas and over here. This year many thousands of tractor operators on the home front will come to close grips with the warning: *Take care of that equipment! Make it last! Make it do!*

Harvester and the International Industrial Power Distributors stand ready to do all in their power to see you through. If your need for new equipment is vital to the war effort, we will have equipment for you. If your need is less vital, we will safeguard your present International Power with every service aid at our command.

INTERNATIONAL HARVESTER COMPANY
180 North Michigan Avenue   Chicago 1, Illinois

Fight with your blood— Give to the Blood Bank
Fight with your money— Buy EXTRA Bonds
Fight on the food front— Stay with that War Garden
Fight the hidden enemy— Fight INFLATION!

INTERNATIONAL HARVESTER
Power for Victory

SUCCESSES AND FIRSTS

The Model K6 was used as a troop hauler.

POST-WAR SUCCESS — FARM AND INDUSTRY

1940 brought the announcement of K-1 through K-5 International trucks, graceful and modern looking. Military commitments, however, consumed most of the production.

I'll go into deeper discussions of how IH's truck and tractor businesses surged after the war in later chapters, but I'll touch briefly on both now. Once domestic production resumed full time, the 1947 KB series was announced with a lot of chrome. It was well received. The International triple diamond logo was prominently displayed on the new bullet-nosed chrome grille.

By 1949, the price was still only $1,350 for the KB-1 pickup. The three-speed transmission shift was now on the steering column.

The heavier and updated KB-5 was quite successful during its 1947-1949 production. Popular use was with grain and stock bodies. Other uses included dump, panel-stake and coal. Over 64,000 KB-5s were built.

The 1948 KB-2 Pickup   Worldwide Vintage Autos

14   SUCCESSES AND FIRSTS

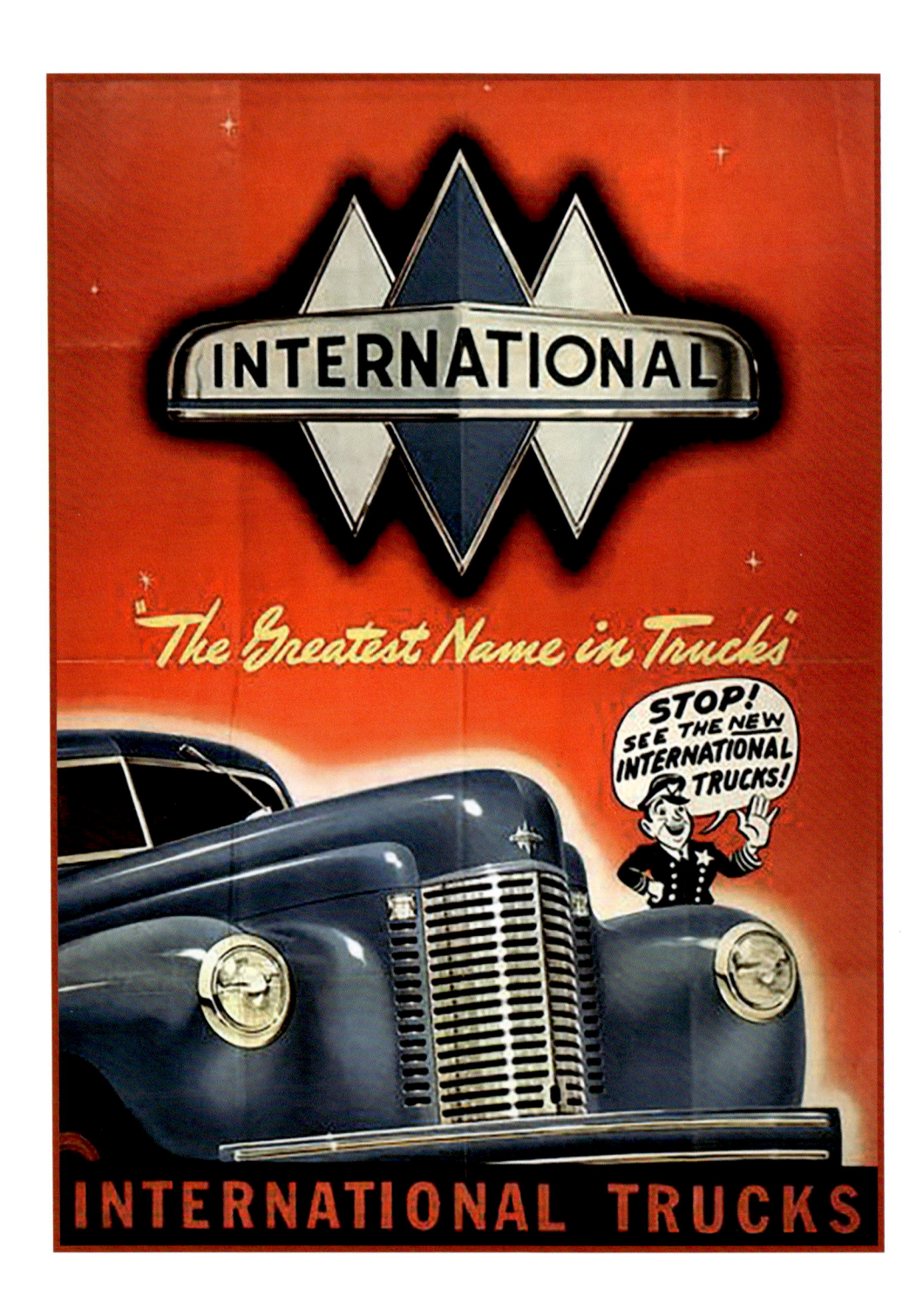

This 1940 D300 was one of the earliest delivery vans. It was larger than others on the market.

SMALL TRACTORS — BIG DEMAND

No one forecast the huge acceptance for a new generation of small tractors created by IH. Released in 1939, the Farmall A and B had immediate demand from small farms and vegetable operations. The Farmall B sold for $605; the A, slightly less. The A and B were produced at Louisville Works, and by 1947 over 220,000 were in use throughout the country.

The Farmall Cub, released in 1947, was a big step forward in tractor power. Its revolutionary size opened another market for IH dealers. The eight-horsepower, four-cylinder tractor was perfect for many agricultural jobs. The engine was offset to the left giving the driver clear vision forward for cultivating.

Soon after its release implements were developed for many jobs including cultivating as well as plowing, planting, mowing, and snow removal. The three-speed cast-iron transmission was easy to shift and extremely durable.

The Cub had no competition for years.

The original Cub was produced from 1947 until 1954. Sales exceeded 180,000 units by 1954 and continued strong over the years. By the late '50s, the Cub remained virtually unchanged except for more horsepower. From the beginning, the Farmall Cub was an "industry first" and a big success for International Harvester.

The 1947 Farmall Cub

In 1950, International Harvester created eye-catching, bright white demonstrator tractors decorated with gold stars. Farmall Cub and Super A, B, and C models were offered to dealers who were urged to "take the Farmall show on the road. Stop at every house. No farmer can resist the temptation to take a look... It's a natural door opener for your salesman to tell the Farmall story. Start country-canvassing today!"

A BIG STEP IN A NEW DIRECTION: REFRIGERATION

In 1945, IH President Fowler McCormick announced a $225 million postwar expansion plan. He used part of that investment to buy a plant in Evansville, Indiana, and started producing freezer chests. Later, refrigerators, air conditioners and dehumidifiers were added.

His reasoning was that these products would be popular with IH farm customers, who had been using Company cream separators since 1907 and dairy coolers since the mid-'30s. Many farms had just received electricity thanks to the rural electrification projects in the U.S. before and after World War II. Orion Samuelson, featured in Chapter Eighteen, vividly remembers the day in 1947 that electricity arrived at his family's Wisconsin farm. Their first purchases included a milking machine, and a cooler so they no longer had to place milk cans in water to keep them chilled until they were picked up. IH also made walk-in freezers for produce and meat.

Harvester engineers were given the funds to develop the refrigeration product line properly, and they created colorful and durable products. Decorator refrigerators were marketed in a big way.

The farm community liked these appliances and bought them in quantity — but the rest of the population did not. The Company tried to establish urban outlets in the late '40s without success. The large appliance companies were too entrenched.

In 1955, IH sold the Evansville plant to Whirlpool for $19 million.

Most agreed that the IH appliances were extremely well designed and well built. They were durable and trouble free. Possibly, if more attention had been given to marketing and distribution, the product line would have prospered.

AUTHOR'S NOTE: Following a year as an apprentice mechanic at our local IH dealership, I moved to the job of salesman in 1953. Most of my sales were related to farm equipment, but Saturdays, when most farm families came to town, I stayed in the showroom to sell refrigeration products. They were popular with our farm customers. Some of these appliances are still working!

SUCCESSES AND FIRSTS　19

ON BOARD THE GOOD SHIP "HARVESTER"

The "Harvester," one of two iron ore ships the Company owned

Another war-related "industry first" involved the Great Lakes. Harvester was the only truck and farm equipment manufacturer to haul ore on its own ships to its own foundry. This was especially advantageous during the WWII steel shortage when IH converted much of its production to military vehicles and armament. Two ships, the "International" and the "Harvester," hauled ore from Superior, Wisconsin, iron mines to the Company's Wisconsin Steel Mill in Chicago. The ships also hauled ore, coal and limestone throughout the Great Lakes from 1911 through 1965.

During the summer of 1953, Reginald Schroeder was a deck hand on the "Harvester" and has experiences he clearly recalls today, 68 years later.

"We were in fog so thick you could not see but only a few feet ahead. Our captain decided to drop anchor and wait for the fog to lift. It was night and many of us were sleeping when the alarm bells rang. I remember waking up and running out on deck. Another ship had not dropped anchor and passed us so closely we could have stepped from our deck to theirs. Everyone was thankful we didn't collide as both ships would have sunk."

Another vivid memory for Schroeder was an accident in Chicago. An inexperienced tug boat captain failed to keep a cable tight and "Harvester," with 8,000 tons of ore aboard, rammed the dock. The jarring collision damaged the bow badly. He's never forgotten how that impact felt.

The "Harvester" in dry dock for repairs after the collision described above by Reginald Schroeder

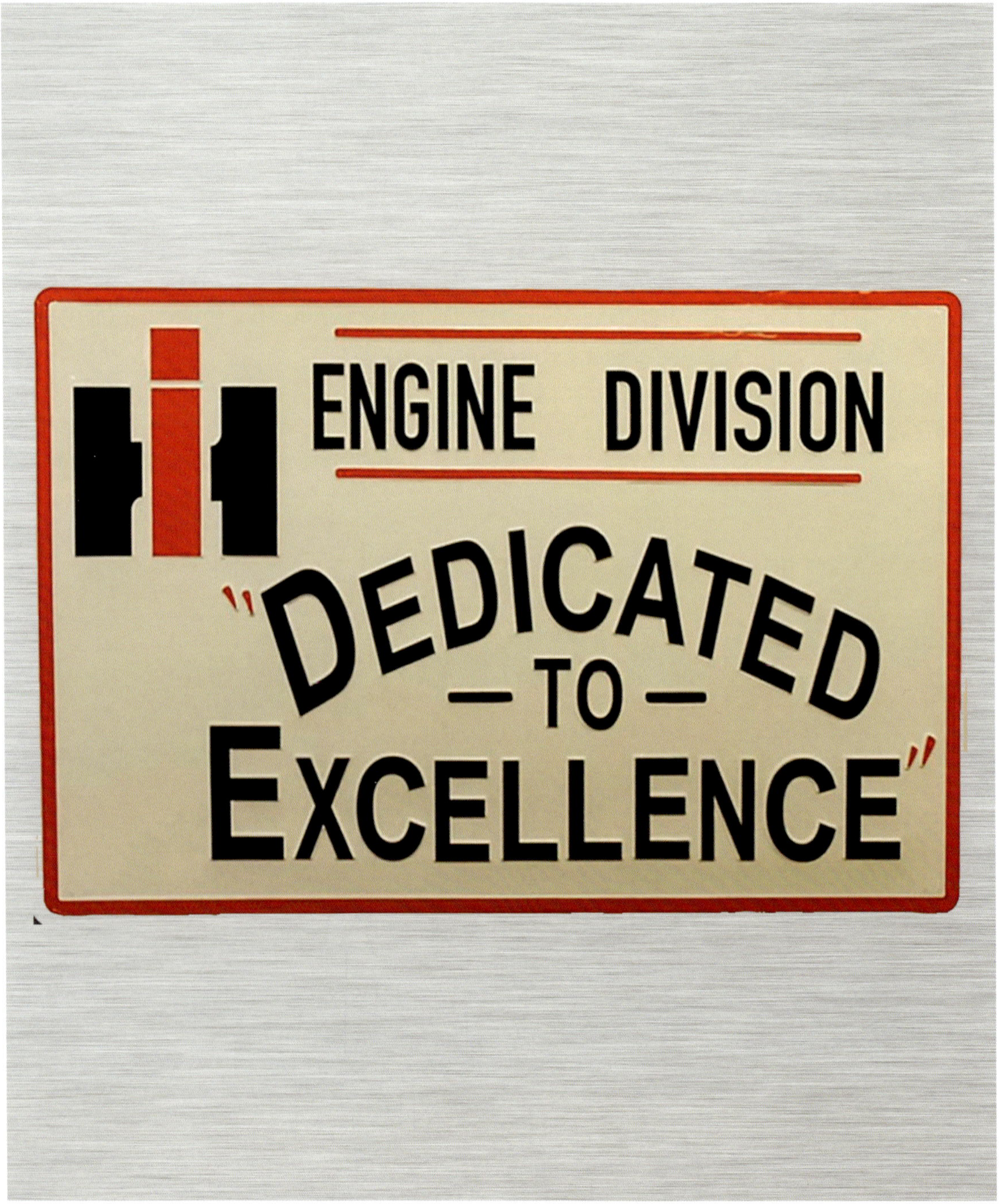
ENGINE DIVISION
"DEDICATED
— TO —
EXCELLENCE"

CHAPTER TWO

ENGINE DESIGN — ONE OF HARVESTER'S GREATEST ACHIEVEMENTS

It's hard to argue with those who rank design and development of engines as the Company's number one accomplishment. After all, without the strength of those engines, how successful would IH's iconic agricultural and industrial machines have been? During this author's 17 years as a dealer with both truck and farm equipment franchises, I don't recall hearing a negative customer complaint about IH engines. Their quality made our job as a dealer much easier.

Dating back to International's vertical engines of 1905, IH engineers designed and manufactured dozens of stationary engine models which were used in many different applications. As this book is focused on the years 1940-1980, we will use just the following examples of stationary engine production and the quantities built.

Model	Years built	Number made
LB	1941-1948	86,000
U-6 & UD-6	1940-1950	25,000
UD-14A	1946-1957	20,000
UD-9	1940-1949	21,000

These IH stationary engines were highly regarded for their durability. They were used in irrigation, sawmills, factory lines, OEM, and many more places.

Farmall Works in Rock Island, Illinois, was a huge producer of engines, both stationary and for wheeled vehicles. Engines for the Company's trucks, farm equipment and construction equipment were also designed internally.

During the '40s, the Diamond series engines used in International trucks were a good example of reliable and quality design. Diamond series engines (Green, Blue, Silver, Black and Red Diamonds) were used in K-line pickups and some larger models. Blue Diamonds were the principal power in K6 and K7 models.

Red Diamond engines had much to do with the success of the KB-8. Engine designs for tractors and implements were equally reliable with long life.

Blue Diamond engine announcement

Red Diamond engine announcement

THE RIGHT ENGINE AT THE RIGHT TIME

Ron Hahn, my friend for many years, worked for IH before joining a large and successful International truck dealership in Illinois. He was very familiar with an IH diesel engine that magazine editors started calling a legend — the DT466 — described as the right engine at the right time.

Hahn praised the DT466 for its reliability and longevity. It was used in industrial and agricultural equipment and trucks. Built at Melrose Park, Illinois, it continued in its original design from 1971 until it had a major transformation in 1993 due to tightening emissions regulations. The engines were redesigned to use electronically controlled unit-direct fuel injection. Various iterations of the DT466 are still in production at Navistar as the MaxxForce DT.

The DT466 instantly developed a reputation as a workhorse with early versions featuring a turbocharger mounted at the top. The industrial and agriculture engines often had the top-mounted turbos, while trucks usually had low-mounted turbos.

Reams have been written about the performance of the DT466 in its many applications. Without question, it is an IH success story!

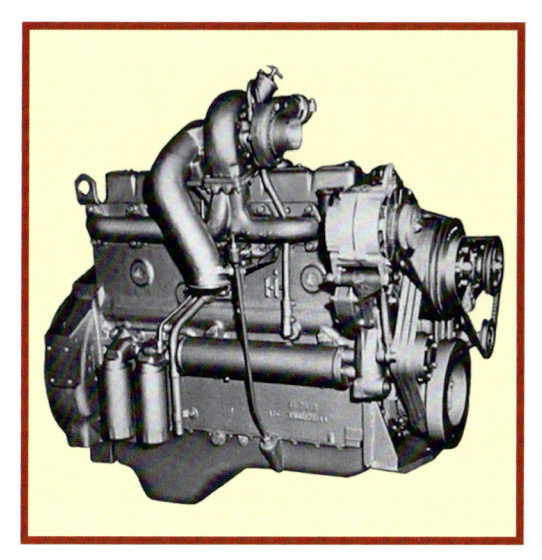

*DT466 with top-mounted turbo (left)
and with the bottom-mounted turbo (right)*

HYDROSTATIC TRANSMISSION

Closely related to IH's success in engine design and development is the development of a variety of transmissions to fit the job. If you want to get a farm implement owner talking, ask about his machine's transmission. It's one area where owners are quick to compliment or criticize, and this transmission got consistently high marks.

In the early '60s, IH Engineering began developing a transmission that would require no shifting. A CVT (Continuously Variable Transmission) or hydrostatic drive that IH engineers developed consisted of a piston-type hydraulic drive powered by a piston-type hydraulic motor.

In 1960, Harvester purchased Solar Aircraft Company, and the experimental hydrostatic drive was installed in a gas turbine developmental tractor, which was then called the HT-341. The gas turbine motor was discontinued but the hydrostatic transmission entered production as part of the 656 tractor introduced in 1967.

The transmission was instantly popular and was added to other models such as the 826. It later became available in all IH combines.

1968 combine with the industry-first hydrostatic drive

CHAPTER THREE

INTERNATIONAL TRUCKS — OUT IN FRONT

1941-46 K8

During the 1950s, the Interstate Highway System opened new roads, and long-distance hauling grew sharply. International Harvester had anticipated this and was prepared for a booming truck market. Throughout the decade, IH assembly plants produced over 60 models of trucks with a variety of wheelbases, engines and transmissions.

Ad for the 54-inch IH tractor cab

AN INDUSTRY FIRST — 54" CAB

When states created length limits, Harvester developed a cab-over-engine series which quickly became dominant in the Class 8 (GVWR over 33,000 lbs.) market. Harvester had discontinued production of cab-overs during WWII, but new models were introduced in 1950. The one shown in the ad on the previous page was the first in the industry to have a cab length under five feet. Models were soon added that were two feet longer. This simplified maintenance by making it easier to access radiator, battery, oil filters and air filters, and the extra room inside the cab allowed for sleeper models.

Ron Hahn sold fleets as well as individual trucks during his long career with IH and an independent dealership, and knows International truck history. I asked him to comment on some of the most successful and industry-leading truck models during years he was in the dealership. Here are his comments:

"One area in which International trucks were very successful and dominant was the cab-over market. IH was early with the shorter cab-over models. They then went a step further and produced the mid-range cab-over named the Cargostar. It was virtually by itself in that market, and did extremely well."

By 1963, International trucks held 35% of the highly competitive heavy-duty market. With more dealerships than others, International owners could expect service wherever they were.

Overseas production of International trucks remained very substantial for many years.

The Transtar II pictured on the following page with a twin trailer/cab-over configuration guaranteed the most freight carrying capacity given the strict length limits at the time. The Transtar series had a large and successful product run from 1968 till 1980.

International stayed on the cutting edge, changing most heavy models to diesel and was experimenting with gas turbines for a time. When certain jobs required specialized trucks, many customers turned to International first.

    The K and KB trucks ushered in the modern era of International trucks. Big military use of these models during WWII established their reputation as being tough and durable. The L series in 1949 carried on that reputation, followed by the R models in 1953 as Harvester provided a large variety of sizes, engines and transmissions. No other company offered as many choices.

Transstar II Cab-over and Twin Trailer

A market where International was very successful was grain trucks. Once again, the variety of models, engines, transmissions and features made them the first choice on many farms. The 1950 model L-180 series pictured above was a workhorse that offered GVWs from 17,000 to 21,500 pounds. It was the predecessor of other lines, including the Loadstar, pictured below, which IH built from 1962 to 1978.

SUCCESSES AND FIRSTS

AUTHOR'S NOTE: Our dealership at Belvidere, Illinois, relied on grain trucks for a substantial part of our business. The trucks shown below were new each year, rented to a canning company and seed company in the spring, then sold to farm customers in the fall: a win for the canning company, a win for the farmers and a win for our dealership. Many additional stories could be featured here about successful International truck models through the years. I've chosen only a few of the most popular.

The Loadstar lineup at Wallem International in 1976

CHAPTER FOUR

CONSTRUCTION EQUIPMENT

IH had attempted to develop a crawler tractor in 1918, but it wasn't until 1929 that the first production model appeared as the 10-20 McCormick-Deering Tractor. Even though not apparent at the time, this crawler launched Harvester into the construction equipment business. Throughout the 1930s, crawler development for construction use expanded rapidly, and by the '40s, the T-6, TD-6 and TD-9 were on the market. After IH successfully built a large quantity of crawler tractors for the military in World War II, Fowler McCormick chose to expand the Company's participation in the construction equipment market. $30 million had been earmarked for manufacturing crawlers, backhoes, forklifts, earthmovers and off-highway trucks. A government-owned aircraft engine plant in Melrose Park, Illinois, was purchased for that production.

That was the beginning of the IH Construction Equipment Division. By the time the T-9 and TD-9 production ended in 1956, 58,182 were in use.

THE BIG RED MACHINE

Caterpillar had taken a firm hold of the construction equipment market, but IH trumped it with a big "industry first." In 1947, the Melrose Park plant started producing the largest tractor in the industry. Called "The Big Red Machine," it was the biggest crawler to enter the market. With a 180-horsepower engine and an eight-speed synchromesh transmission — another industry first — it outperformed Caterpillar's D-8 and out-powered it by 10 horsepower. Thousands of TD-24s were sold and it was instrumental in the creation of the interstate highway system, which was authorized by the Federal Aid Highway Act of 1956. IH made the TD-24 until 1959.

IH continued to expand its earthmoving division by buying companies and technology. Its heavy tractor line was already established. Next came the purchase in 1952 of the Frank G. Hough Company, builder of an iconic machine named the Payloader. This highly successful family-owned company employed 3,000 in Milwaukee. International Harvester was on a mission to compete with Caterpillar.

In 1956, IH introduced the Payhauler line of off-highway rear-dump trucks with 25-ton capacity. In 1964, the Payhauler 180 entered service. This 45-ton truck became the first all-wheel drive, end-dump truck of that size in the world. Another industry first!

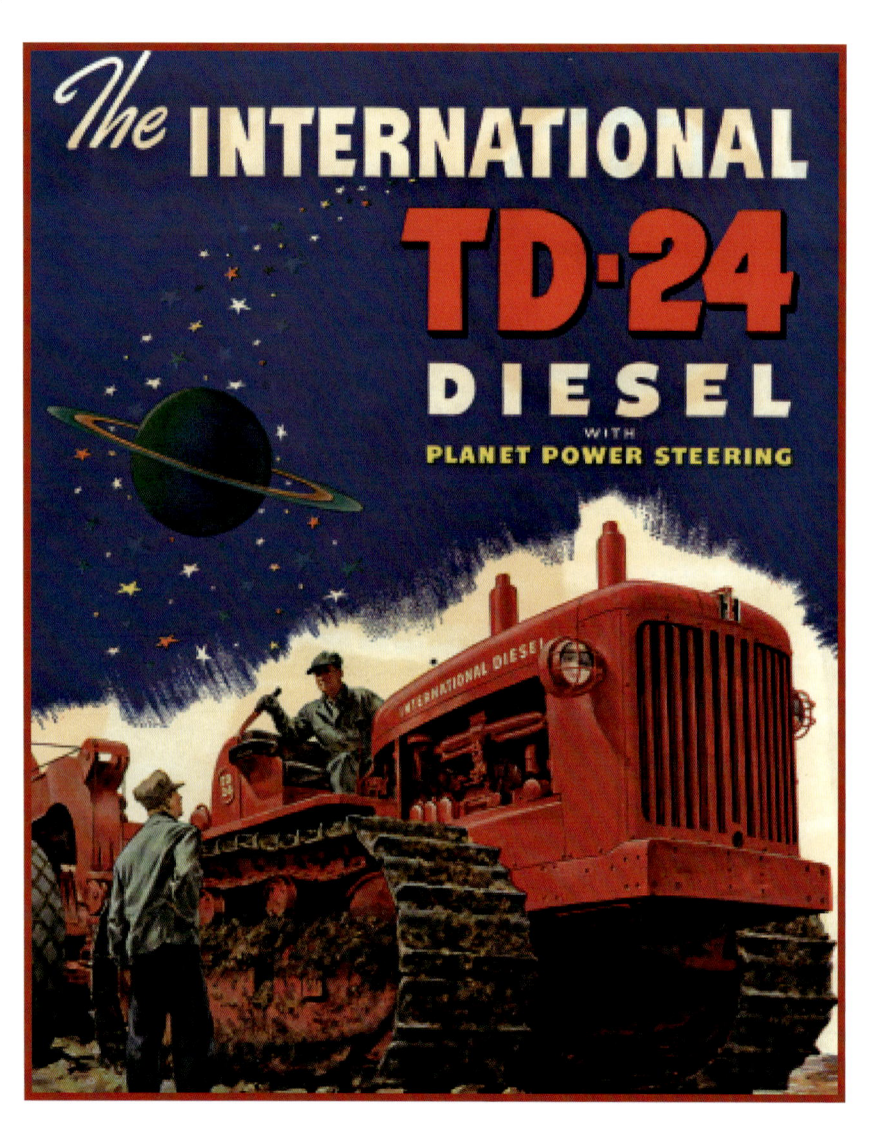

SUCCESSES AND FIRSTS 35

A variety of matched equipment is made for the TD-24 by leading manufacturers with years of experience in this activity. Mounted equipment is developed by these allied equipment specialists working with International engineers. A combination of tractor and equipment that is well balanced for maximum traction and safety results from this close coordination. Pulled equipment is designed in sizes for most profitable use of the tractor's power and speed. The TD-24 and matched allied equipment are your best bet for any job.

IH CONSTRUCTION EQUIPMENT and MOTOR TRUCK PROJECT
GLEN CANYON DAM

Glen Canyon Dam became the second largest concrete arch dam in the U.S. It backs up Lake Powell, Arizona.

Under construction from the mid-1950s into the '60s, it was a huge project involving IH Payhaulers and trucks. The winning contractor already owned 60 Model 95 Payhaulers from their work on the St. Lawrence Seaway. For the Glen Canyon project, they obtained 22 additional Model 95 Payhaulers, 11 TD-24 bulldozers, numerous R-195 tractors with tank trailers, plus pickup trucks and Travelalls for ambulances. A unique feature of the 45-ton Payhauler was the dual front tires that allowed the load to be distributed evenly across both axles.

The Glen Canyon Dam project was completed in 1966. The rest of the decade and the '70s brought mixed results for the division.

In the early '80s, IH needed cash. The Payhauler line was sold to employees in 1982 and the Construction Equipment Division was disbanded in 1983. Shortly after that, in 1984, the rest of the Hough operation was sold to Dresser. Just like that, Harvester was out of the construction equipment business.

IH cornered the off-highway dump truck market with its Payloader and later the Payhauler. First built in 1956 as a rear-wheel drive capable of carrying a 25-ton load. Later versions were all-wheel drive with 45- and 50-ton ratings. Early models had a Detroit Diesel 16V71 engine, and later models switched to Cummins engines.

38   SUCCESSES AND FIRSTS

IH equipment played a major role in the Glen Canyon Dam project.

CHAPTER FIVE

TILLAGE TOOLS RATE A BLUE RIBBON

During the period of this book's focus, many manufacturers entered the tillage market. University studies had recommended more effective ground-working practices, and farmers were always wanting to update their equipment.

Harvester's engineering department had long been a dream job for many college graduates. A lot of them had grown up on red farms and visualized a career designing farm equipment. Their dads and uncles on the farm always had suggestions on what changes should be made, and Harvester listened, improving disks and plows as a result.

Soon after IH formed in 1902, it put disk harrows high on its priority list. Over 200 different models were built for use with horses and the early tractors. By the '50s, over 350 models of disk harrows had been built by IH. Its engineering experience with these tools surpassed everyone in the industry. During later years and following WWII, IH tools continued to be widely accepted.

Plows were an equal IH priority, also dating back to the early 1900s. In 1928, production began on a model called the No. 8 Little Genius plow. It was built until 1960. Over 67,000 were sold.

Much later, the 700 series

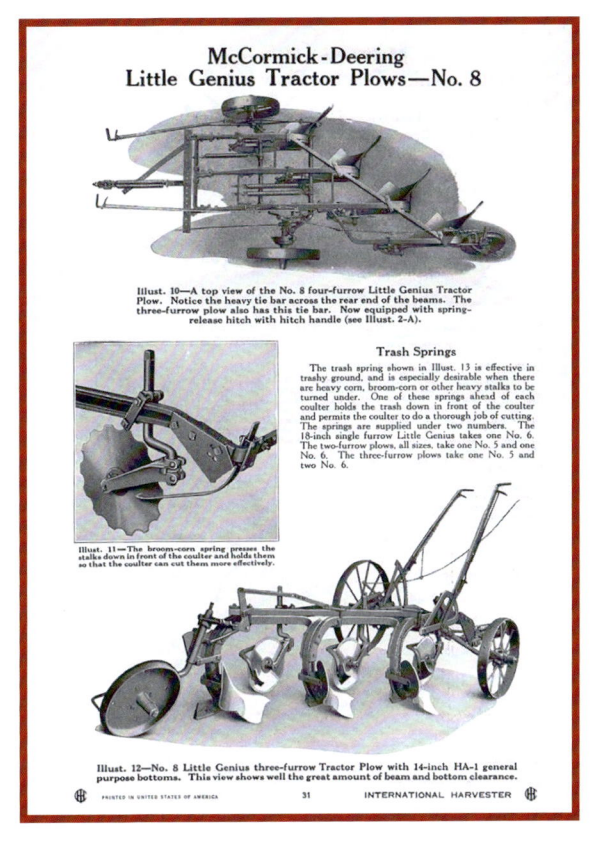

plows and 400 series disks held a dominant place in the ground working market, as well as vibra-shank cultivators and other models.

It would be difficult to pick just one of the many IH tillage tools as an "industry first." The entire line was hugely successful during the years between 1940 and 1980. Truly, a Blue Ribbon rating.

THE RED POSTER CHILD OF TRACTOR PULLS

In Chapter Two, I wrote about the many successes Harvester had developing and building stationary engines. Beginning in 1905, they were used worldwide in many applications, including irrigation, OEM, sawmills, and factory production lines.

The engines' reliability also served IH well in trucks, tractors and construction equipment. Industrial and agricultural users knew the engines would stand up well in tough use and conditions. They earned a reputation for being well built and sturdy.

These same qualities made Farmall tractors constant winners in pulling contests. Pullers would modify the engines to boost horsepower and win contests.

Engine Builder magazine described it well in this article.

> *The Farmall H and M model tractors are popular antique pulling tractors in part because they are inexpensive to purchase and easy to upgrade to make more horsepower. To gain an advantage, you have to do a little homework. International Harvester built various rear end combinations for different tractor applications. The most popular pulling tractor swap is a rear end from a sugar cane tractor that had a low creeper gear in it, a pretty sneaky advantage.*
>
> *Then there is the Farmall engine itself. First, change the cylinder head to one from a Farmall model 400 gas tractor, that is then milled .125", with valves installed from an International 466 tractor, adding double springs and machining the ports for correct alignment. Add an LP (propane) intake manifold milled to match the head and manifold ports. Use a copper head gasket set from an 806 tractor.*
>
> *Then, use a carburetor from a model 400, open the jets up, add a Rocket governor, electronic ignition and run at least 105 octane gasoline. Time*

the governor with the carburetor, with a larger fuel line from the bottom tank to carb. Add an electric fuel pump. This combination will yield 95-100 horsepower, more than double the stock 45 horsepower.

Notice the last line: "This combination will yield 95-100 horsepower ..."

Only a strong and well-built engine can hold together with that increase. The Super M engine did just that.

Photo by Randy Rundle for Engine Builder magazine

Years passed. Production tractor horsepower continued to increase. Tractor pullers continued to modify their tractors. In 1963, the Farmall 806 was announced, and pullers discovered that its 361 cubic inch engine could be greatly modified without blowing up. It became a hit in pulling contests.

Then the 1206 came out, the first turbocharged farm tractor and the first over 100 horsepower. This tractor really caught the attention of pullers, and contests saw an abundance of black smoke from modified 1206s with turbocharged 361 engines. Pullers loved it. So did the crowds.

These were just two of the Internationals that were successful at tractor pulls. Later models continued belching black smoke, exciting crowds and winning blue ribbons. The 1466 was another model that did extremely well.

Today, some call the 1206 the poster child of tractor pulls because of that success. It is now one of the most sought-after vintage tractors amongst collectors.

Photo by Kristi Pine

Jason Schultz of Richland Center, Wisconsin, and his Farmall 1206 at the 2012 Viola, Wisconsin, Horse and Colt Show Tractor Pull

CHAPTER SIX

EXPANSION!

Between 1940 and 1945, the IH employee total had risen from 52,000 to 70,000. That number kept growing throughout the '40s, and the Company was now planning its post-war future under the leadership of Fowler McCormick.

McCormick became Chairman of the Board in 1946. He correctly forecast the huge post-war expansion in the American economy. The nation's gross domestic product (GDP) doubled from 1947 to 1959, and doubled again from 1960 to 1970.

IH COTTON PICKER
TOP FIVE 20th CENTURY AG ACHIEVEMENTS

The U.S. Patent Office issued its first patent for a mechanical cotton picker in 1850. Many attempts were made to create a workable machine. Pneumatic, electrical, spindle, thresher and stripper machines were all tried, and they all failed.

Harvester had a cotton picker about ready to market when WWII began. The project was delayed until 1945. In 1949, IH built the Memphis Works plant for production of cotton pickers. By 1972, most cotton was picked mechanically and International Harvester owned a large share of that market.

In 2000, the American Society of Agricultural Engineers (ASAE) recognized the IH cotton picker's excellence by naming it one of the top five agricultural achievements of the 20th century.

ANOTHER GREAT SUCCESS

By the end of 1949, the Farmall H had become first in number of tractors built of one model. In 1953, when its run finally ended, 391,730 had been produced. To this day, it retains the top spot for the number of row crop tractors built in the world.

Our neighbor bought a new Farmall M. I was about four years old, and that

44   SUCCESSES AND FIRSTS

A 1957 IH 220A Cotton Picker pictured near Robinsonville, Mississippi

shiny, red tractor was the greatest looking thing I'd ever seen. A few years later, when I was old enough to cultivate with our Allis Chalmers WC, I was even more impressed with the M. The Allis had hand brakes. You had to take your hands off the steering wheel to use them. The M had foot brakes. The Allis was started with a hand crank. The M had an electric starter. All this for $1,440! A lot of neighbors were envious of his tractor, and I was one of them.

A Super H belonging to IH enthusiast and farm broadcaster Max Armstrong is shown in downtown Chicago. The skyscraper directly above the tractor seat was IH headquarters from 1965 until the Company's end.

By the mid-'40s, after the war, I was still in grade school and spending summer days cultivating with our Allis Chalmers WC. Dad planted with a check-row planter. In my opinion, there are few jobs more miserable than cross cultivating corn. The first time is easy. The second time means riding up and down on every row. In today's world, having a kid do this would be called child abuse. In those days, it was just another job that played a part in wanting to never farm when I grew up.

Many will say that the H and M were the greatest successes International Harvester Farm Equipment Division ever had. Given the number of units sold, that would be undeniable. Total number of all models of the M reached 298,219. Together with the H models, nearly three-quarters of a billion were sold!

AUTHOR'S NOTE: *When my friend Hal Beitlich heard I was writing this book, he sent me the following story about his grandfather's 1946 Farmall M. I think you'll enjoy it.*

My grandfather had the area threshing route. This included about eight farms just a few miles south of La Crosse, Wisconsin. The machine was a Red River Special powered by the M. At an early age, I traveled with him on the route each day as he moved from farm to farm. I remember sitting on the M while it was on the belt, watching the belt splice travel back and forth from the tractor to the machine. Grandpa would sit on top of the thresher, watching the process and oiling. End of the day was pack-up time, and we'd move to another farm.

When Grandfather retired, his youngest son, my uncle, took over the home farm. My dad had bought a farm a couple miles from the home place. The brothers started sharing machinery: corn choppers, pickers, wagons, etc., allowing the sharing of harvest effort. I recall chopping silage corn with the M on a Gehl one-row chopper. The lack of a live power take-off and a speedy first gear was a load for the M. It would lug down and down until you had to tap the clutch and get out of gear to allow the chopper to clean out. That was necessary as silage corn was planted very thick. The mighty M worked hard and was very reliable.

ANOTHER INDUSTRY FIRST

In 1952, International Harvester announced the Super M-TA (SMTA) with the Torque Amplifier transmission. It marked the first time the TA was used in farm equipment. It was a revolutionary development in that it essentially doubled the tractor's gear range. The TA reduced the speed in each of the five gears, giving the tractor 10 speeds. It consisted of a precision planetary gear unit that provided a shift-free choice. With the pull of one lever, the TA reduced speed without clutching and shifting to a lower gear.

The Super M-TA Farmall was available with gasoline, diesel, and LPG fuels. In 1954, there were 26,964 M-TA tractors built; only around 500 of these tractors were designated LPG tractors. These tractors were sent to Western Tank and Steel Company in Lubbock, Texas, for the conversion. Many of the M-TAs were then sent to Arizona and were used in the cotton fields.

IH expanded the TA option, offering it with many models through the years. It gave dealers a huge competitive advantage.

> Super M: gear with spark engine
> Super M-TA: TA with spark engine
> Super MD: gear with diesel engine
> Super MD-TA: TA with diesel engine
> Super MV: high-crop
> Manufactured at Rock Island, Illinois
> International Harvester 4.3L 4-cyl gasoline
> International Harvester 4.3L 4-cyl LP gas

48 SUCCESSES AND FIRSTS

Mecum Auction photos
Top: A Super M-TA with an LP conversion. Bottom: A1954 Super M-TA

CHAPTER SEVEN

AXIAL-FLOW COMBINE

THE STAR OF THE FARM EQUIPMENT DIVISION

In the fall of 1977, IH unveiled another "industry first" — the Axial-Flow combine. Its acceptance was immediate and enthusiastic, but most people weren't aware of how long IH had been developing the rotary combine. That's because it had been done in secret at the Fort Wayne and East Moline plants. With John Deere located near the Illinois plant, keeping it under wraps was difficult, but IH was able to pull it off. Access to the research and development area was extremely tight.

R & D on the combine began in the late '50s. As the concept development moved forward, expectations grew that the design could reach production stages within a decade. Instead, it took almost 20 years. Separating corn from the cob had been a far easier task than building a machine that could be adapted to harvest many crops in many different conditions. Seemingly endless challenges were overcome as different crops, using cut grain from local sources, were put through a series of tests on different concepts and configurations until, finally, "the one" was found.

Over a million man hours of engineering work is said to have gone into the Axial-Flow. Other manufacturers had experimented with the rotary concept, but IH embraced it and when the Axial-Flow was introduced, there were two models: the 1440, featuring a 135 horsepower, 436 cubic inch engine, a 24-inch rotor and a 145 bushel grain tank, and the 1460, with a 170 horsepower engine and a 180 bushel grain tank. Later models would add turbo-charged engines, including the iconic DT466, which I write about in other chapters of this book.

Dealers knew immediately that they had a winner. They were selling a combine better than any before. For my 2019 IH book, *The Breakup*, I interviewed 28 IH dealers from all over the U.S. and Canada. Some had held truck and farm equipment contracts prior to 1980 and some had not. I asked each to name the IH product they thought was the best through those years. Thirteen named the Axial-Flow combine. Its innovative design put it out front in the industry, they believed, and its longevity among customers made it a huge sales and service success.

For these reasons, we are crowning the Axial-Flow combine the #1 IH Success and Industry First. And IH's brilliant engineers didn't stop there. The Axial-Flow combine, with its many design changes and improvements, continues to be a major success and industry leader. Almost 43 years later, an auction article in a recent magazine is titled "Red Harvesters Bring More." Auction prices on used models always tell a story.

This is the cover of an advertising booklet featuring the Axial-Flow combine. A faded image in the background shows two men using Cyrus McCormick's reaper of 1831.

SUCCESSES AND FIRSTS   51

This cutaway view illustrates the unique single-rotor design. As the only moving part in the threshing/separating system, this spinning rotor creates a gentle rubbing action that is repeated several times as the crop is moved in a spiral path over a concave and grate area.

AUTHOR'S NOTE: *The secrecy around the design and development of the Axial-Flow extended to field testing. Mike Silberhorn, retired from IH and Cub Cadet Corporation, shares his experience.*

In the mid-1970s, I was an IH Farm Equipment Zone Manager calling on dealers in Northeastern Illinois, south of Chicago. We lived in Joliet, IL. During that time we were riding on the success of the 66 series tractors and the Cyclo planters. We were selling everything we could get our hands on.

I received a call one day in the Fall of 1975, as I remember, from the Quad Cities Regional office. My task was to get permission from a large acreage farmer that was a good IH customer. They wanted engineers to combine soybeans with an experimental combine. I was told to stay away from the machine and the people working with it. The farmer was to keep anything he saw confidential. Mike Rousonelos of Plainfield, IL, a large acreage farmer and loyal IH customer, agreed to let the machine be used on his fields.

On visiting with Mike, I found out that he knew no details on the machine but he knew they would combine for a while, take out the rotor, come back a day or so later, install a different one, and repeat this exercise several times. I had heard scuttlebutt about the development of a new combine, and the temptation to see it was too much. Though I was told to stay away, I went out one night to look at it. It was enclosed with shields and shrouds so that I could not tell if it was much different than a 915 combine. Little did I know then that it was a machine that would so dramatically change the industry, and I am still glad that I could be a very small part of it.

AUTHOR'S NOTE: *This chapter wouldn't be complete without noting the huge role the Fort Wayne Truck Works played in the Axial-Flow's development, a role that remains a source of great pride in Indiana. Ryan DuVall, the founder and CEO of Harvester Homecoming in Fort Wayne, shares the following essay.*

There were a lot of firsts over the years at the Fort Wayne Truck Works but in the late 1970s, there was a first and only that not only somewhat broke the rules for International Harvester, it changed farming forever.

Fearing corporate espionage by nearby rival John Deere in Moline, Illinois, International Harvester devised a plan to build the first five experimental Axial-Flow combines in Fort Wayne.

Those combines were the only agricultural equipment other than trucks built in Fort Wayne during its 80-year run from 1923 to 1983, and the project was special to the folks in Indiana who helped develop them in the Fort Wayne engineering complex.

"It was an exciting project for all of us," said Fred Stinson, the Engineering Shops supervisor in Fort Wayne at the time. "And it was the highlight of my career for sure."

Stinson, who spent 32 years with the company starting in 1961, recalled visiting International Harvester's East Moline, Illinois, combine plant ahead of time to, "just get a general feel about the project and see how they did things up there. It was totally unique to us."

The company's top engineers were stationed in Fort Wayne, but they were truck experts. So Stinson, who spent 32 years with the company starting in 1961, and Fred Wiegel, one of the mechanic/assemblers at the time, did some recruiting within.

"We were fortunate to have a fella in maintenance who had once worked for a farm equipment place in Payne, Ohio, who knew a lot more about them than we did," said Wiegel, who spent 43 years at the Fort Wayne Truck Works. "So, we pulled him out and he worked on them which was good, because we didn't know anything about them."

The wooden floor of the prototype buildup section was jam packed with big red harvesting machines for months, and the project was so important, a third shift was created to get it done. And when it was done, it was done right.

"The final drive was casted here, engineering fine-tuned them in the machine shop, and we assembled them in the Axle-Transmission Lab," Stinson recalled. "It was a project that had the whole Engineering Department behind it."

Though it was supposed to be a big secret, there was no hiding the big red machines once they were built.

"We actually oiled them up and took them out to Road Test (the Proving Grounds test facility) to test them out," Stinson said.

The five prototypes were shipped to Texas to start the real field tests, and three of the five were returned to Fort Wayne afterward so they could be altered into display models. Windows were installed along the flow so folks could see the new technology at work.

Once the project moved on, Stinson and Wiegel said, calls would occasionally come in from Moline with questions for the build team. Those calls filled the Fort Wayne engineers with pride because it verified how advanced and ahead of the pack the Fort Wayne team was.

Courtesy Harvester Homecoming, Inc., Fort Wayne, Indiana
One of the five Axial-Flow prototypes built at the Fort Wayne Truck Works that would be sent to Texas for field testing. Notice the lack of markings, part of IH's efforts to keep the project under wraps and away from the prying eyes. This photo was taken behind the Fort Wayne Truck Works engineering center.

SUCCESSES AND FIRSTS   55

After field testing in Texas, three of the combines were returned to Fort Wayne Works for installation of windows for people to see the inner workings. These photos were taken in the Prototype Buildup area of the Truck Development and Technology Center (Engineering) in Fort Wayne. The gentleman shown is the late Walter Domer, a 34-year veteran of IH. Photos courtesy Harvester Homecoming, Inc., Fort Wayne, Indiana

HE KNEW IT WAS REVOLUTIONARY

Tom Taylor spent 45 years in Harvester's East Moline Combine Works. He started there in 1959 and retired as Materials Handling Superintendent in 2004.

During the early '70s plant rumors were all about a secret project in a remote part of the plant. It was off limits and restricted to everyone but the crew involved. Years passed. Finally, instructions came to begin a production line changeover to a new model. A great deal of advance work was completed before the orders came to begin production. As the changeover evolved, Tom and his crew realized this was not just a routine update. And when the new model was unveiled, it was clear to him that this was a revolutionary change. And it turned out that he was right!

Roy Hummel of Milk River, Alberta, was an IH dealer and remembers well when the Axial-Flow arrived.

> The most influential development that International Harvester made in my time as a dealer was the introduction of the Axial-Flow combine in 1977. In 1975, my brother-in-law Dale Baldwin and I purchased the IH dealership called Madge Equipment and had 715, 815, and 915 conventional combines to sell. In the fall of 1976, my uncle Paul Madge, whom we bought the dealership from, came to the shop and said he'd had a call from an old friend and customer named Merle Van Winkle. Merle was a custom combine operator and his annual harvest route started in the southern wheat country and ended at the Canadian border. Merle's claim was that so far in his career, he had purchased over 100 IH combines, and that was years before custom harvesters traded their whole fleet every year. Many of the IH prototype combines and engineers accompanied Merle on his annual run. His trade name was "Rip the Reaper."
>
> On the phone call, Merle told Paul, "You have one chance to come to the field north of Cut Bank, Montana, and see the most astounding, revolutionary prototype combine I have ever operated. This combine will make IH a leader in the combine business." The next day, four customers and Paul and I loaded into my IH Travelall for the journey to Cut Bank.

There were no model numbers on the combine, but Merle was a navy vet and had nicknamed this one "Queen Martha" due to the appearance of the rear platform. There were several of these prototypes being tested that fall.

The rotor side doors were padlocked on this future Model 1440, but we could get some visual of the mechanics of this combine by looking above the sieves from the rear of the machine. This view revealed the simplicity of this combine. Merle attested to the increased productivity over the 915 combine, especially as you pushed the combine faster in a heavy swath, and particularly in barley. I was struck by the ease of settings in a variety of crops.

In those days, IH would gather 12 to 15 dealers in a territory together in the fall for an annual ordering allotment. I don't remember for sure, but I believe there were 200 Axial-Flow combines available for 1977 for all of North America. Since Alberta is 760 miles long, IH wanted to locate one in the north, another in central Alberta, and the third one in the south. As the summer of 1977 approached, it became evident the first available 1440 combine in Alberta would go to the dealer that sold it first, not the dealer that wanted it the most.

We sold the first Axial-Flow combine in Alberta to Verdigris Farms, operated by Hovey Ken Reese, who had accompanied us to Montana to view the first prototype, and was our farm neighbour three miles to the east. This was the first piece of agricultural equipment I knew of that had a buddy seat, and now every self-propelled machine has a buddy seat. The seat was in the Axial-Flow combine to enable training of new operators and became very useful in demonstrating the combine to potential customers. It helped us convert numerous John Deere owners. At the time, I believe the IH North American combine market share was around 15%. Within three years, we were ordering 20 combines at a time and our local market share rose to 60%.

One story from that first year of the Axial-Flow is a testament to what a revolutionary product it was. A farmer in Fairfield, Montana, grew malt barley on contract for Coors Brewing Company. The people at the Coors elevator knew nothing about this new rotary combine, and when they received their first truckload of malt barley that fall, they contacted the farmer and told him he wasn't required to clean the barley before delivering it.

HAY AND FORAGE

IH equipment for these crops dates back to 1907 with a horse-powered hay press. The Company continued as a serious contender in the hay and forage market with the 1940 introduction of the No. 15 pickup baler. First models were powered by a belt drive, as shown in the photos on a following page, and later versions had a small engine to power the baling mechanism. It was used as a stationary baler where the hay was hauled to it or, quite often, the baler was pulled through the field to piles created with a dump rake. One man fed hay fed into the baler with a pitchfork. Another man tied the bales.

The 50-T and 50-W series balers were built from 1944 to 1952. Memphis Works built 8,000. The PTO-driven No. 45 was built from 1954 to 1957. It was replaced by the No. 46.

The larger 55-T was produced from 1953 to 1959, was capable of six bales per minute. Over 13,000 were sold. It was also offered as a wire-tie, and 16,000 were sold.

The 1970s brought out the No. 37 baler, a modern and compact machine. Later in the decade other models were added: the Nos. 420, 430 and 440.

Forage harvesters received a lot of attention from cattle owners after WWII. Over 10,000 No. 2 ensilage machines came out of the factory from 1945 to 1952. Then a more modern No. 20-C, followed by the No. 15 and No. 50 were produced during the late '50s, and the No. 650 during the '60s. International Harvester had greatly accelerated their activity in this market.

The '50s and '60s brought a host of new short line companies producing hay and forage equipment. It became a highly competitive market. Some IH models were more successful than others, and IH dealers always had a product to sell.

In their extensive collection, Ron Knight and his son Brian of Great Casterton, England, have two IHC No. 15 baling presses circa 1939-1949. One belt-powered stationary baler, above, and one pickup baler with an on-board engine for use in the field. Note that operating either is a two to three person job.

Dave Kleine of Cedar Lake, Indiana, restored this 1948 50T. It's powered by a four-cylinder Continental engine with a hand crank starter.

Illust. 2
Left front view of the 37 Twine Baler.

SUCCESSES AND FIRSTS   61

McCORMICK®
No. 46 BALER
POWER TAKE-OFF OR ENGINE DRIVE

Extra capacity to <u>outbale</u> them all

Many vintage manuals like this can be found at www.agrimanuals.com.

No. 15 IH single row silage/hay chopper, circa 1970, restored by Dave Kleine

CHAPTER EIGHT

THE 2+2

In 1970, International Harvester began experimenting with putting two tractors together. In January 1979, the 2+2 was introduced. Above is a 1981 3388 2+2 at the 2015 Red Power Round Up.

It was a huge rollout! Farm equipment dealers nationwide traveled to Phoenix late in 1978 to attend International Harvester's gala announcement of the 3388 and 3588 tractors, what it called the "2+2" series. The master of ceremonies was Orion Samuelson and entertainment was Herb Alpert and The Tijuana Brass. In January of 1979, the 2+2, the first-ever articulated row-crop tractor came on the market. Market research had indicated that with the front section steerable and the back section (with the driver) unchanged, operation in row-crop conditions would benefit. IH added the 3788 in 1980.

The two models ranged from 111 to 126 drawbar horsepower (DBHP). The 3788 came out in 1980 at 142 DBHP.

From day one, the tractor was controversial. Many years later in 2018 when I interviewed dealers for my IH book *The Breakup,* they recalled their reactions when the 2+2s were introduced. Here are a few:

* *From a Southern dealer:* "It was ahead of its time. We sold several and they worked well. We believe the 7288 and 7488 prototypes would have been successful."
* *From a Midwest dealer:* "Ugly tractor." He sold a few but pivot points gave trouble.
* *From an Eastern dealer:* "Interesting, but clumsy. We sold two."
* *A Saskatchewan dealer said,* "We were impressed with the 2+2. CaseIH should have kept it in the line. (He has two in his collection.)
* *Another Canadian dealer* recalled laughing when he saw it for the first time at the Phoenix rollout. He stared as it kept coming — and coming — on stage. He thought it was the longest and the ugliest tractor he'd ever seen. But his dealership sold quite a few.
* *A Deep South dealer* had only this to say: "Horrid, weird, not reliable."
* *And one from a Midwest dealer:* "Had no luck selling the 2+2. It was too revolutionary."

Between 1978 and 1984, combined sales of 3388, 3588 and 3788 models totaled 10,285, a poor performance when compared to a single tractor, the 2WD 1466, which had sales of 25,264 during the same period.

A 1982 introduction of the 6388 and 6588 models replaced the older 33 and 35s, with the 6788 replacing the 3788 in 1983. Total sales of the new "three" was 1,261, cut short by the Tenneco purchase of IH and the termination of the 2+2. Pre-production of 7288 and 7488 models totaled 36 units before the CaseIH merger.

A 2014 *Successful Farming Magazine* article looked back at the 2+2 from an historical perspective. Author Dave Mowitz commented that the once-maligned and misunderstood 2+2 is now looked upon in more favorable terms by collectors at auctions. The article went on to say that the tractor was a victim of corporate mismanagement but was successful in its first year of production with nearly 3,000 sold, over one-fourth of the total 4WD market. But the following year, 1980, began a downward trend of purchasing due to factors including high interest rates.

Photo by Jim Allen

Prospective buyers driving a 2+2 for the first time often felt unsettled when the front section turned but the cab didn't. It wasn't what they were accustomed to. However, if they had the opportunity to operate it for a few hours, they became more comfortable with it, and the advantage of the design in row-crop situations became apparent.

There will always be disagreement about the CaseIH decision to terminate the 2+2. Some feel that the 7288 and 7488 could have succeeded with power shift.

The 2+2 was another industry first, however, another example of Harvester Engineering willing to try something new. Like the Scout. And the Cub Cadet. And a really big step ahead with the Axial-Flow combine.

Photo by Jim Allen

The hood on a 1980 3788 slides open for access to the DT466 engine.

CHAPTER NINE

A SMALL TRACTOR TRIUMPH

The first mockups of the Cub Cadet were called the Cubette. This photo of one of the first prototypes was provided by former IH designer Keith Burnham, who was part of the team that designed the Cubette, which became the Cub Cadet.

No one in the Company forecast this little tractor becoming such a big success, and so quickly!

In the late '50s, the IH Product Planning Group recognized a new and growing market for small, four-wheeled tractors with air-cooled engines, seven to 10 horsepower, suitable for mowing and blade work.

Advanced Engineering Group at Farm Equipment Research and Engineering Center (FEREC) began development of such a tractor. *Product Committee Report 31* dated February 1960 spelled out the market for a tractor in the $500 range.

Engineering progressed rapidly with design that year. The decision was made to use Farmall Cub parts wherever possible to keep the price down. Use of internal brakes and the Cub three-speed shaft-driven transmission helped a lot.

Following committee discussions, testing and changes, the pre-production Cub Cadet was approved. At first, it was called the Cubette because of the use of the Farmall Cub parts. Someone suggested the name be Cub Cadet, and that's the name that stuck.

The original 1961 Cub Cadet sales brochure

The Product Identification Committee had recommended both red and yellow tractors be produced, red for ag dealers and yellow for industrial franchises. The Divisional Product Committee eliminated the red option. (That option would come up 19 years later.)

Twenty-five Cadets were produced initially and sent to the Southern U.S. where mowing season was underway. An overwhelming positive response encouraged the Company to release the Cub Cadet for production, beginning in January 1961.

International Harvester had become the first farm equipment manufacturer to build and market its own line of garden tractors. The Cadet had an advantage over other brands because of the Cub transmission that was not only sturdier and more reliable, but gave the Cadet a big-tractor feel. A slow-speed IH Danco Underdrive "creeper" gear could be added for three extra-slow speeds.

The first Cadets in 1961 were powered by a seven-horsepower Kohler engine only. More powerful engines came in 1965. A wide variety of tillage and maintenance attachments made the Cadet even more attractive.

- Garden plowing became common with a one-bottom, 10-inch moldboard plow.
- Other tillage tools included a six-shovel cultivator, rotary tiller, disc harrow and peg-tooth harrow.
- Front blade for clearing snow and grading
- Snow thrower and rear-wheel snow chains
- Seeder/fertilizer spreader
- Lawn roller and lawn aerator
- Reel mower, lawn rake and lawn sweeper
- Hammer knife mower
- Rotary sweeper
- Mounted power sprayers became popular in orchards.
- A sand trap rake made golf course maintenance easier.

First Year Sales Forecast	5,000 units
First Year Actual Sales	24,000 units
First Five Years Actual Sales	49,000 units

Early sales exceeded goals, and total sales of IH-produced Cub Cadets: 683,782!

AUTHOR'S NOTE: *Keith Burnham, a retired IH designer living in Leland, Michigan, was working at Harvester when planning for the Cub Cadet began. His drawings led to the Cubette and then the Cadet. His son Jim shared a conversation with his dad about working at IH and how his designs led to the production models.*

What my dad accomplished was extraordinary in that he wasn't an official Industrial Engineer with IH; he never had formal higher education training in any of it. He cut his teeth at Lockheed Martin in the '50s and gained hands-on, practical designing experience that allowed him to do things better than many of the "more pedigreed" engineers IH had.

Dad did a lot of blueprint sketches and 3D mockups on the larger tractor models, but it wouldn't have been good if HQ knew he was doing that kind of work. Fortunately, he had allies in high places. Here's one of this memories:

"The responsibility for styling was with the World Headquarters Industrial Design Department in downtown Chicago. They would come out to the Hinsdale office to visit us once a week, and would wander from desk to desk to desk. Just before one of their visits, my boss, Pierce Richardson, saw my color drawing of the Cub Cadet on my drafting table. He took it to his office and hid it under his ink blotter because he didn't want World Headquarters knowing I had been working on the design. Well, I went looking for it, found it, stole it back and put it back on my desk. Pierce was livid, but I had some allies higher up. The World Headquarters people were getting ready to go to Louisville to set up the Cadet program, and my boss's boss's boss saw the drawing on my desk. He held it up and said to the group, 'I don't care what the Cub Cadet looks like as long as it looks like this.'"

SUCCESSES AND FIRSTS   71

SKETCH - CUB CADET WITH BUMPER TYPE SEAT SUPPORT & FENDERS
K.W. BURNHAM 10-5-60

Above (1960) and below (1963) are two of Keith Burnham's many drawings of the Cadet. The drawing below is the one referenced by the IH exec in the story from Keith's son, Jim.

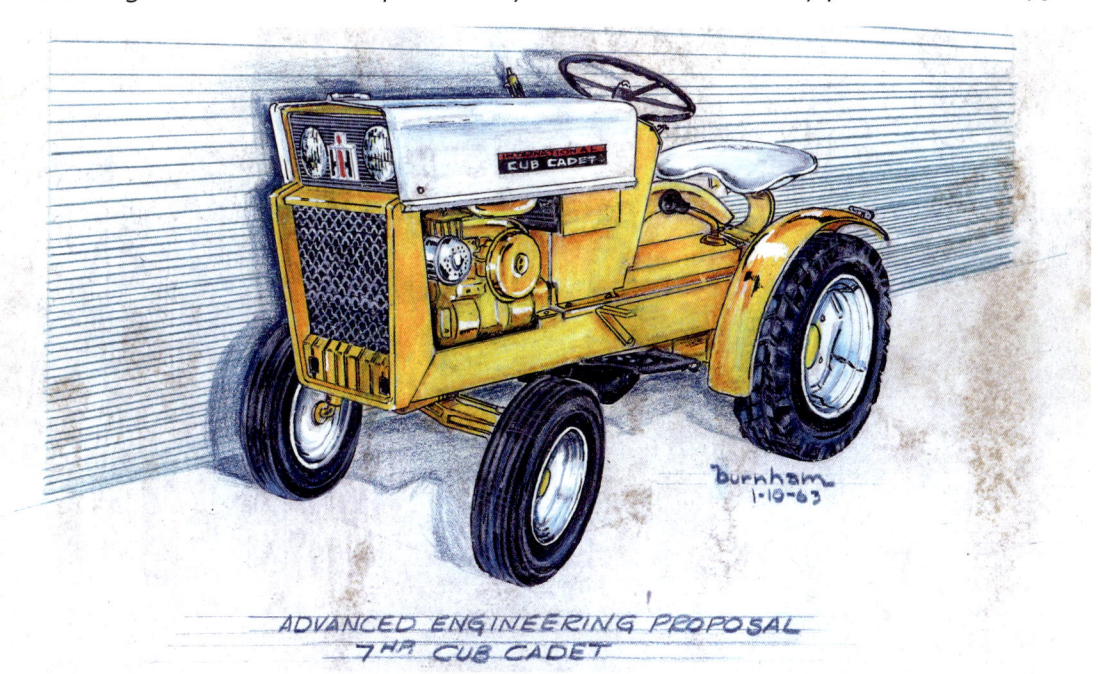

Burnham 1-10-63

ADVANCED ENGINEERING PROPOSAL 7 H.P. CUB CADET

THE CUB CADET GROWS UP

From 1960 to 1980, multiple Cadet models were added, with power options increasing from a seven HP Kohler engine to a 19.9 HP Onan twin-cylinder. In 1979, the 982, pictured below, debuted. It was 6 1/2" longer and 6" wider than the original.

After the sale of the product line to Cub Cadet Corporation, Harvester dealers would continue to buy inventory from IH and the color would be red. All other outlets would receive yellow and white tractors.

The Cadet 982

The author introduces a new model Cadet to dealers at Hickory Hill. c. 1964-65

The prototype Cub Cadet Hydro. Sundstrand, Inc. of Rockford used an original seven-horsepower Cub Cadet. They invited IH engineers for a demo. IH approved it and in 1965, the Model 123 with a 12 HP engine became the first direct-shaft driven hydrostatic drive garden tractor. It completely changed the riding mower industry.

PULLING CONTESTS

It should be little surprise that the company which produced tractors that dominated pulling contests for decades saw similar success with the garden tractors it built. Ever since garden tractor pulling contests started, the Cub Cadet was a star. National pulling contests began in about 1993 and the larger horsepower Cadets were consistently among the winners.

AUTHOR'S NOTE: My involvement with Cub Cadets spanned 25 years. First was the introduction of the newly-announced Cadet line in 1961. I was Product Knowledge Supervisor for the Madison, Wisconsin, IH district office, and introduced the Cadet to our dealer organization in Green Bay's City Stadium, home of the Packers. Next came national responsibility for all Louisville Works products, which included Cub Cadets. Later, I bought an IH dealership in Belvidere, Illinois. The dealership was close to Rockford, and we typically sold 50 Cadets or more each year for the 17 years we had the store. I'll conclude by saying I've cut my lawn for all these years with a Cadet, and still do!

The Cub Cadet was a family affair for the Wallems. Left, Stephen poses for an ad for the 1976 Bi-Centennial Cadet.

Right, son Jeff is at the wheel and daughter Linda is right behind in the 1970 Belvidere Fourth of July Parade.

CHAPTER TEN

SOMETHING TO REPLACE THE HORSE

The chief designer at IH, Ted Ornas, was told in the late 1950s to design "something to replace the horse!" It was to be a tough off-road vehicle to compete with the only other vehicle of its kind, the Willys Jeep. In only 24 months, what Ornas recalls as "an heroic achievement considering the concept was unique and no in-house engine or manufacturing was available or even considered when the program started," a vehicle was born.

His team came up with the precursor of the more sophisticated IH 4WD vehicles to come, and set the stage for the influx of SUVs over the past two decades.

They named it the Scout.

Proof of this vehicle's success? A total of 532,674 sold from 1960 to 1980.

The first early 1960s models were pickups, available in both 4X2 and 4X4 wheel drives. The 152 cubic inch four-cylinder engine was the right bank of a 304 V8.

Then came an enclosed cabin, and later the 304 V8 and 345 V8. The much improved Scout II was released in 1971. It was a versatile and reliable off-the-road vehicle as well as being comfortable, with an automotive interior and a sharp, stylish appearance.

Various versions through the years included Shawnee, CVI, Selective Edition, Spirit of '76, Patriot, Midas Edition, Special, Monteverdi Safari.

The 1976 Scout

The 1977-79 Scout Traveler

Jerry Boone drove his 1977 Super SSII (Super Sport) to victory in the tough Baja 1000 California-Mexico Race. He raced his stripped-down Scout to finish two hours ahead of his nearest competitor.

The Scout III SSV concept vehicle was scheduled to replace the Scout II in 1981. This ended with IH's decision to discontinue Scout production on October 21, 1980.

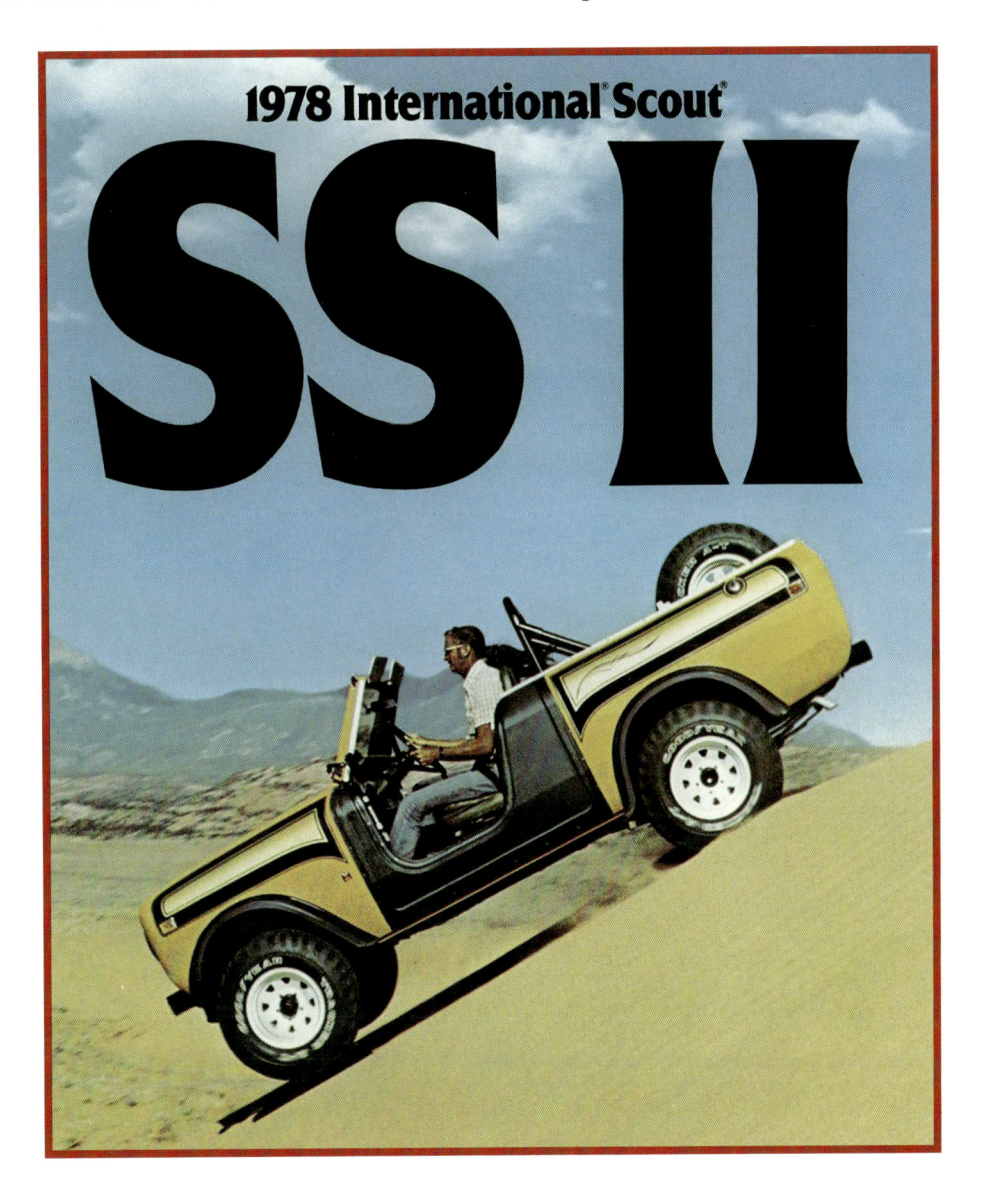

AUTHOR'S NOTE: *I bought our Belvidere, Illinois, IH dealership in 1969. We had both farm equipment and truck contracts. Pickups, Scouts and Travelalls were a substantial part of our business. My teenage son worked at the store and drove a tired, high mileage Scout 800 for a short while until it was in the shop most of the time. His Scout II was a much better vehicle, solid and comfortable. Here are his recent comments about his two Scouts.*

"SCOUTING" THE SUV TREND
by Jeff Wallem

Some years back, I struck up a conversation with a gentleman seated next to me on a flight. At one point, he talked about "sooves" and it took me a few moments to figure out he was describing a sport utility vehicle.

Growing up with a father who was an IH executive and later an International Harvester farm equipment and truck dealer, I have many memories of time spent in the tough Scouts and Travelalls long before the term "sport utility vehicle" was widely used.

In high school, my first "car" was a red and white '65 Scout 4x4. With a 152 cubic inch four banger engine (1/2 of an International 304 V8) and a non-synchronized three-speed manual transmission, it was the most basic transportation. That Scout taught me a lot about what could go wrong in an old machine. IHC had various parts and service programs promoting the "Uptime" availability of its products. My Scout, though, with an old Myers snowplow mounted, somehow seemed to experience more "downtime" when the snow fell.

The Scout 80 was too slow for an inexperienced kid to get into much trouble speeding but, of course, I found other ways to do just that. There was the time I took it off-roading in a plowed field along with my friend Gary, who had one of the original Ford Broncos. We both got stuck and Dad pulled us out with a tractor from his dealership.

My next Scout was a really nice '72 Scout II with the 304 V8. It was a big improvement in terms of reliability and design but was still able to teach me a few things. I did not know that even a 4X4 can get stuck on a sandy beach if you do not let some air out of the tires!

While most guys my age were into muscle cars or sports cars, these early sport utilities were doing a lot of work and providing a lot of fun while teaching kids like me many useful lessons. It would be years before SUVs transformed the automotive market. There's no question Scouts were ahead of their time.

The Travelall, lower left, the Scout, to the right, the Light Line pickup above it, and the Travelette club cab (an industry first) at top. The pickups, Travelall and Travelette were discontinued in 1975, and the Scout in 1980.

The 1953-54 R-110 Travelall

BLAZING THE TRAIL

When it comes to industry firsts, there is no disputing that International Harvester engineers created the first four-wheel drive sport utility vehicles long before they would be called SUVs. In 1953, the successful K-Series pickup chassis was also being used under a panel body for airport people movers. When the R-Series light truck chassis went into production, the panel vehicle was given more windows, a third door, and the Travelall was born! The first models were two-wheel drive, but 4WD came in 1956, which opened up a big market for customers in off-road businesses and sportsmen. The 4WD Chevrolet Suburban didn't come on the scene until 1960.

The Travelall had windows all around and rear seats. Either two or three rows of seats were offered. A wagon-style tailgate was an option. In 1958, a third door was added. The fourth door was added in 1961, 12 years before the Suburban's fourth-door model. The Travelall by IH was a step into the future, and was sold in big quantities by its dealers until it was discontinued in 1975.

CHAPTER ELEVEN

IH IN THE '50s
Working for the Company

At an IHCC chapter meeting in 2019, a fellow asked me why I'd chosen to work at Harvester, and what it was like. He wondered why I had not gone to work at Allis, because I had mentioned that I grew up on a WC.

Since then, I've thought more about it. I'm convinced now that seeing our neighbor's new Farmall M, and how impressive it was, convinced me to try to get a job with our local Harvester dealer instead of the Allis dealer.

Our high school let seniors out of school at 1 p.m. if they had a part-time job that was considered apprentice work. I qualified because the dealer was making me a mechanic's apprentice, and I worked there from 1 p.m. till 5 p.m. daily.

My job was scraping paint off tractors that were about to be repainted. My other important job was emptying waste cans. Next, I became a helper assembling the 2M mounted corn picker. They arrived from the factory with the side panels removed. We centered the bolt holes in the sheet metal with a punch to get the bolts started. I'm surprised I still have all ten fingers.

I didn't know it at the time, but that picker would be a great success. The leader in the mounted picker market, it was more efficient, operated at higher speed through the field, and was a perfect match for the Farmall M that it was first mounted on. There were slight changes and upgrades made over the years with the 2ME, 2MH, and 2MHD.

Between 1939 and 1952, over 43,000 were sold. I hope none of those I worked on came apart in the field.

Our local dealership became a company-owned store when International Harvester bought it. I kept working there part-time while in college, and it led to me being a summer intern for the Company in 1955. At the end of the summer, I was told I would have a job after graduating from the University of Illinois.

That summer of '55 was a fun one. I helped zone managers with odd jobs

Photo by Dave Kleine

The 2MH picker mounted on a 1953 Super M

such as driving equipment displays at county fairs, etc., across the state of Illinois. I worked for the Broadview District Office, which supervised IH activities in Northern Illinois. I vividly recall one event. A demonstration was planned on a Dwight, Illinois, farm. A new 101 combine had to be moved from the Elburn dealership to the farm.

Elburn is on Route 47, over 50 miles north of Dwight. The destination farm at Dwight was also on Route 47, a busy two-lane highway. The zone manager dropped me off at Elburn and said he would pick me up later at Dwight.

The 101 combine was over eight feet wide, and took up the entire southbound lane. Top speed was 12 mph. Traffic was, and is, always heavy on that road. The minute I pulled out on the highway to start south, the horns started blowing. Traffic stacked up behind me, and I could only occasionally find a spot wide enough to pull over and let traffic pass. So for five hours, I drove straight ahead and listened to

> Corn heads make a McCormick No. 101 or 151 right at home in the cornfield. Symmetrical design and row-matching tread let the big drive wheels straddle two rows squarely... center the separator for easiest steering. Ideal weight distribution puts 80% of the weight on the drive wheels for best traction. The engine is high, out of the trash and dust for longest life, lowest fire hazards. Rear axle extensions (special) let guide wheels straddle rows.

From a 1959 IH publication

horns, horns and more horns. The model I was driving had a cab and, as all of them are, it was tall enough to stand up in, so I took turns sitting and standing, trying to ignore the horns and the hand signals from passing drivers. I can still hear the horns all these years later.

In 1955, many counties had fairs, and IH dealers displayed at most of them. A frequent job for me during that summer internship was demonstrating the newly-announced IH Electrall power generator. It was created to provide tractor-mounted AC electrical power for small jobs on the farm and in industry.

The dealer would have a tractor-mounted Electrall at his display, and I would spend the day plugging in an electric razor and shaving, or drilling holes in a board with an electric drill. Just the noise of the tractor running would always draw spectators, and we talked to them all day about the Electrall. I shaved often enough that summer to last for years.

The Electrall was an innovative device that drew a lot of attention, but was

SUCCESSES AND FIRSTS

The IH Electrall sales display

ahead of its time. Its success was limited, and possibly would have had better market acceptance in later years. It was discontinued.

Good news came at the end of the summer of '55, when, as promised, IH management advised me that upon graduation from college the following spring, I would have a permanent job with the Company.

My first job after my 1956 graduation was assistant zone manager (in earlier years it was called blockman). That lasted only two months before I left for a two-year tour in the army. Harvester, to its great credit, counted my two years in the service as employee time for pension purposes. Like so many instances, the Company was great to work for.

During the two months I was on that zone, the dealers were conducting field days to give customers a chance to drive the recently announced Farmall 400. After 16 years of Farmall M production, IH replaced it with the 400 which had over 35% more power. Everyone likes more power on the farm, and those field days were fun. One of the dealers I worked with was in Belvidere, Illinois. Little did I know I would buy that dealership 12 years later.

After my two years in the army, IH sent me to central Wisconsin as zone manager, calling on 22 IH dealers. Every winter, many dealers held an open house and invited farmers and their families to their store for free lunch, displays, discounts, and movies. As zone manager, it was my job to show IH-branded movies that were made for just this purpose. I still remember the names of some. "Getting Old Red Ready" and "Helpful Henry" were two I'll never forget. My audiences were dairy farmers in the vicinities of Beaver Dam, Waupun, Newburg and others.

The open houses were good for the dealer and for IH. The customers always had questions about when new equipment was coming out, particularly hay tools.

The Farmall 460 and 560 had been announced just before I moved to Wisconsin. The 460 sold very well across the state.

In 1960, I was transferred to the Madison District Office and became supervisor of Product Knowledge. One of my jobs was to motivate zone managers and dealers with selling points demonstrating the superiority of the 560D vs. the John Deere 4010. One campaign I prepared focused on fuel consumption, shown on the following page.

We helped the dealers conduct competitive field days and I recall renting a John Deere 3010 and hauling it to dealer events all over Wisconsin. Field day guests would be invited to drive the 460, then drive the 3010 because it was hard to figure out the shift pattern.

One night, as my team and I were traveling to the next day's field test, I was east of Wausau, Wisconsin, hauling the 3010. It was dark and something flashed into my headlights, followed by a cloud of steam that obstructed my view. I had no idea what had happened, and slowed to a stop right in the middle of the road. The other two members of our team were following behind me and ran up to see why I had stopped.

The source of the dark flash and the steam became quickly apparent. The radiator had been penetrated by the leg of a deer. It had jumped in front of my truck and the impact was so forceful its leg had torn off. We walked back up the road and found the rest of the dead deer lying alongside the road.

We parked the truck and trailer on the siding, and next morning picked up a new radiator from the dealership, installed it, and arrived to the field test on time.

The IH 2-point hitch was demonstrated at these events and at the county fairs. Ultimately, the industry standardized on the 3-point hitch design and abandoned the 2-point hitch. Harvester got a lot of good years out of the 2-point design, however.

One of my motivational comparisons for IH salespeople

CHAPTER TWELVE

A NEW JOB – AT WORLD HEADQUARTERS

In April 1964, I was assigned to World Headquarters in Chicago. The job was National Sales Supervisor for products produced at Louisville Works and agricultural crawlers from Melrose Park Works.

The first day I reported for work at 180 North Michigan Avenue is hard to forget. I had driven in from Peoria the night before and checked in at the Knickerbocker Hotel. It was an ornate luxury hotel that played host to many dignitaries, including Presidents Kennedy and Nixon, and the Rolling Stones. It once had a casino in the penthouse run by the Capone family, but it was long gone by the time I checked in.

The next morning, I walked south from the hotel along Michigan Avenue amidst a sidewalk full of other folks going to work. Even though I had been on this street before, this time it was different. Men all wore hats, suits and ties, and no one made eye contact. I was part of this new world, and it felt strange for a boy who grew up on a dairy farm. It was April Fool's Day 1964. I'd never been in the 24-story building before. The elevator took me to the eighth floor, where I was greeted by Harvester management, many of whom I had met at the district offices when they'd visited.

I would typically spend each Monday in the office and travel nationwide the rest of the week. That job lasted until April of 1966, when I was assigned to the job of Farm Equipment Export Manager, Overseas Division. At that time, Brooks McCormick was managing the division and it was my first opportunity to work directly under his supervision. My first encounter with him was at World Headquarters.

Brooks was a great-grandnephew of Cyrus Hall McCormick. His Yale roommate was Henry Ford II, and each was best man at the other's wedding. They rose to head two of the largest U.S. companies.

I worked for Peoria District Manager Lawrence Barnett during 1962-63. He often talked about his experiences working with Brooks when they were beginning their IH careers at Kansas City. Barnett described Brooks as fully committed to his career, putting in long hours with everyone else, and always downplaying the importance of his family name. I had the same impressions when I worked under Mr. McCormick in 1966-68.

IH published a report in the mid-seventies entitled *IH Farm Report — Agriculture at a Crossroads*. These quotes from Brooks McCormick appeared in that special edition:

> *"The nation is going through a period of emotional reaction against foreign trade. This attitude is usually justified as 'protecting' America against foreign imports. But when we put up walls against foreign trade, our trading partners are going to put up walls against us."*
>
> *"We know from past experience how our trading partners would react, or over-react, if bills like the Burke-Hartke are passed. If we shut out their radios they will shut out our soybeans. The retaliation is likely to fall on farm commodities because that is one of our major areas of trade surplus."*

Brooks was a strong advocate of free trade and continued to speak out in its favor throughout his career. He worked long hours up to the end of his presidency, trying to keep International Harvester independent.

When I chose to resign from Harvester in 1968, Mr. McCormick accepted my resignation and wished me well. When I told him I planned to be an IH dealer, he asked that I work 30 more days and help him choose my replacement, but told me I should take whatever time was needed to decide on a location for the dealership and make arrangements for its opening.

Brooks was elected president of IH four months after I left and was the last McCormick name to head International Harvester. He served as president from 1968 to 1978. Presidents with the McCormick name that preceded him were Cyrus Hall McCormick, Cyrus Hall McCormick Jr. and President/Chairman Harold Fowler McCormick.

When he retired in 1978 and devoted time to managing his farm near Warrenville, Illinois, we leased equipment to him. He expressed his ongoing belief that IH would continue to supply dealerships with trucks and farm equipment.

BROOKS McCORMICK'S CAREER
International Harvester Company

- 1945   General Superintendent Melrose Park Works
- 1947   Assistant Works Manager, Melrose Park Works
- 1949   Kansas City Assistant District Manager
- 1950   Dallas District Manager
- 1951   Joint Managing Director Great Britain
- 1952   Managing Director Great Britain
- 1955   Director of Manufacturing Parent Company
- 1957   Executive Vice President, International Harvester
- 1958   Elected to Board of Directors
- 1968   Elected President and Chief Operating Officer
- 1971   Elected Chief Executive Officer
- 1978   Elected Chairman of the Board
- 1980   Retires from Chairman and from IH

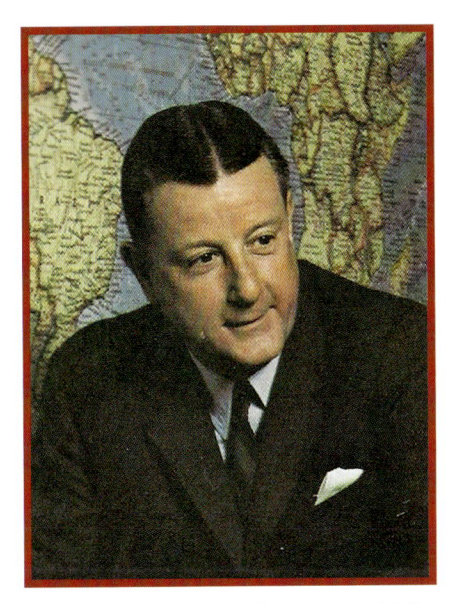

Brooks McCormick, 1917-2006

1965 IH GENERAL OFFICE CHANGES LOCATION
A NECESSARY CHANGE

Harvester had headquartered at 180 North Michigan Avenue in Chicago (pictured above) for 28 years. Fourteen-hundred employees over-filled the space, and a move of the general office had been planned for two years. To assure a smooth flow of corporate business, the move had to be accomplished over a weekend.

Several of us left our offices at 180 on Wednesday, November 11, 1965, to go to Hickory Hill Farm, the IH facility at Sheridan, Illinois. We had IH dealers arriving Thursday and Friday for a new product announcement.

Monday, November 15, I went to work in a different location — the new Equitable Life Assurance Building, 401 N. Michigan Ave. It was home to the new world headquarters of International Harvester.

Adding extra significance to the move: The Equitable Building was built on the original site of Cyrus McCormick's reaper factory. He built it in 1849 and it operated till the Chicago fire destroyed it in 1871.

Harvester would occupy 12 floors in the new building. Fernstrom Storage & Van Company had hauled 130 truckloads beforehand, and 133 additional loads on

With only a weekend to complete the massive move, night work was a must. While most of the city rested, the 12 floors IH occupied were lit up and busy.

November 12 and 13. Fifteen thousand boxes were moved three and a half blocks up Michigan Avenue that weekend.

Valuables, such as securities, deeds, abstracts, cash and traveler's checks, were packed and stored separately, secured over the weekend by the Brinks Company.

Fernstrom provided 152 employees and Harvester had 52 staff members assisting the move. It was a short move but what a difference in buildings! The new offices had huge windows with great views.

We were accustomed to long waits at the elevators in the old building. All 1,400 employees would usually arrive at similar times. This photo shows employees arriving the first day at 401. The large bank of elevators swallowed us quickly.

My office was on the 15th floor. A staff member handed me a printed layout of offices, and I found mine on the west side overlooking Michigan Avenue. What a view! The most amazing sight was the Wrigley Building clock. It was across from my window and looked huge! (I've never had that big an office clock before or since.)

The Equitable Building is on a large courtyard adjoining the Chicago River on the south side and Tribune Tower on the north side, with Michigan Avenue at the front door. It was a great place to work.

This massive move was so well planned and carried out, that it deserves to be considered as one of the Company's success stories.

The following year, I joined IH Export Company. That meant a move from the 15th floor up to the 26th floor.

I quickly learned that a low cloud layer over the Loop in Chicago meant the 26th floor would often be above the cloud layer. In sunshine. How strange it was to leave home on a dark, overcast morning, ride the commuter train down to the Loop, walk to the Equitable Building and ride the elevator up to my office in sunshine!

That happened often, particularly in spring. My family came to visit my office once, and it was that kind of day. All these years later, they talk about the sunshine on the 26th floor!

FORT WAYNE MOVE

Also deserving to be considered as one of International Harvester's success stories was the move going on at the Fort Wayne, Indiana, truck plant at about the same time as the general office's move. Like the GO, IH's largest truck plant had also outgrown its quarters. In Fort Wayne's case, the "move" meant expansion and modernization: the total rearrangement of a factory and its assembly lines. Demand for trucks was steadily climbing; production couldn't be halted. IH considered building a new plant, but that would be too costly. Instead, the truck makers provided a plan that involved a complete renewal of the existing plant whereby, in theory, at least, not a day of production would be lost.

The old "A" and "B" assembly lines turned corners in three places and as the number of truck models and variations grew over the years, production became more and more inefficient. So, the plan to pull out the old lines and install one long line took shape, and the planners met their goal of not losing a day of production. On top of that, a state-of-the-art paint booth was added.

One interesting comparison between the general office move and the factory update: The distance from the old general office to the new one is about a third of a mile. The length of the new "A" assembly line was 1,662 feet — about a third of a mile.

Engineers used made-to-scale cutouts to plan a new assembly line.

SUCCESSES AND FIRSTS   95

The new streamlined assembly line

FARMALL
FARMALL
QUALITY EQUIPMENT
SOLD HERE
McCORMICK
FARMALL

CHAPTER THIRTEEN

COMBINE SQUARE DANCES

During the 1950s and '60s, Harvester used tractor square dances as entertainment at customer events. Tractors, generally the latest models IH was promoting, were Do-Si-Do-ing to the square dance caller and band.

In 1962, we entertained visitors at Wisconsin's Dodge County Fair in a different way. We square danced with combines! The IH 91 combine had just been released for sale. It featured a lever-controlled planetary steering system that allowed the combine to literally turn in its own tracks. Perfect for square dancing and for demonstrating the 91's maneuverability.

After practicing ahead of time with the three 91s, the drivers performed throughout to the sound of square dance music. It drew standing-room only crowds

An IH sales brochure focuses on maneuverability.

several times a day. Just about everyone left the fairgrounds knowing about the new IH 91 combine.

FARM PROGRESS SHOW

Every year, hundreds of thousands of farmers, ag marketers and farm equipment manufacturers convene at the annual Farm Progress Show. Customers come to be both informed about new equipment and entertained.

A favorite among attendees at the Farm Progress Show was the Farmall 504 square dance.

At the 1963 show in Peoria, between presentations about the new 706 and 806 and performances by the Sage Riders, we brought back the tried and true crowd pleaser: the tractor square dance team. This time I used four Farmall 504s, each with a square-dancer "face" attached to the grill. The arena was jammed with spectators for each show.

The team responsible for the IH exhibit at this show consisted of the eight zone managers and the service department personnel. We started preparations 10 days ahead of the show, built an arena, set up a large tent full of displays, and tested the equipment that would be demonstrated in the fields. Bad weather and wind were always a worry, and we hoped for sunshine during the three-day show. Sound equipment for display presentations and arena shows was a challenge because the generators providing power for lighting in the tent as well as public address equipment made a lot of noise.

A key to success at farm equipment shows is to stand out. We did that in 1963 by renting a balloon to draw attention to our display. All was going well until a member of our Chicago management team came to the site and found out the balloon had hydrogen in it, not helium. Hydrogen is cheaper than helium, but is quite explosive! He directed me to fly the balloon at a much higher altitude to increase the safety buffer between it and the crowd, which we did.

It still drew the crowds.

Dealers throughout the country responded enthusiastically when the 706 and 806 models were announced. A lot of farms had grown in acreage, and one more plow bottom was needed. It had been five years since the 460 and 560 were brought out. Sixty-six thousand 560s were in use, and over 33,000 460s. The 706 and 806 brought a real boost in power. The 806 provided 85 DBHP versus the replaced 560 with 53 DBHP. The smaller farmer with a 460 at 36 DBHP could jump up to a 706 with 65 DBHP.

Dealers conducted field days to put prospective buyers in the seat of the new tractors. The seat, controls and gauges were all more modern. Comments heard from farmers at field days in our Peoria area included that these new tractors were "more fun to drive." 706 and 806 sales were strong during their lifespan. Approximately 51,000 of each model were sold.

100 | SUCCESSES AND FIRSTS

The hydrogen balloon drew big crowds to our Farm Progress Show booth.

SUCCESSES AND FIRSTS   101

The 806, shown above, and the 706 were the first all-new designs from IH in about 30 years and they came at a perfect time in the company's history. We had a new CEO, Harry Bercher, who directed engineers to build a tough tractor to challenge the JD 4020, and they came through. The 806 was marketed as "The toughest tractor ever built." Many thousands of customers who bought the 806 between 1963 and 1967 would agree with that claim. It was definitely an IH success!

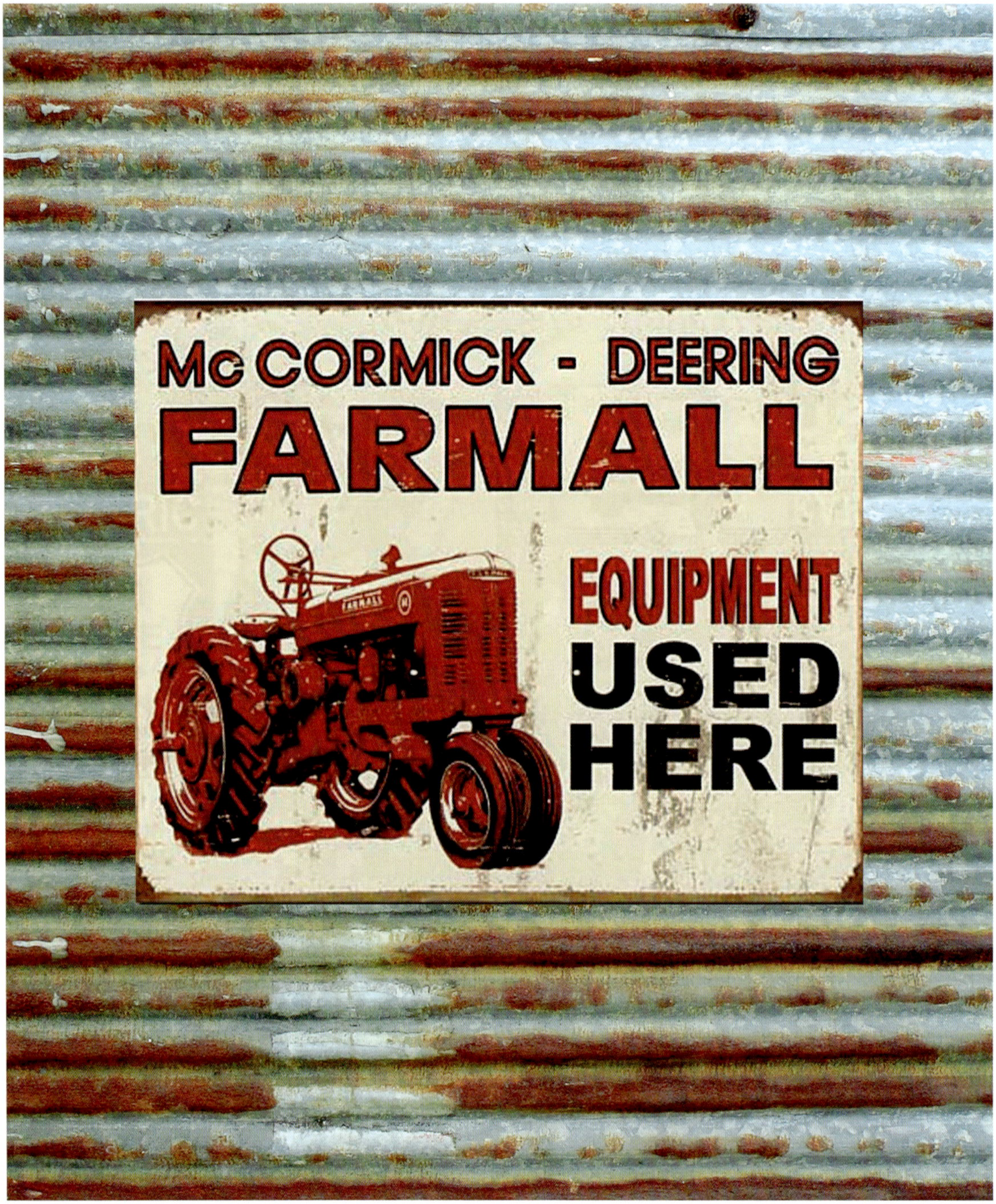
McCORMICK - DEERING
FARMALL
EQUIPMENT
USED
HERE

CHAPTER FOURTEEN

A PERSONAL FIRST

In 1969, I purchased a dealership in Belvidere, Illinois, through the co-dealer plan. This IH program made it possible for me to obtain the dealership as a minority shareholder with Harvester, then buy out their shares from profits. This worked out well for me and for many others throughout the country.

It was an exciting time for my family. Instead of traveling much of the year worldwide, I was home every night. I had observed many dealers building their own business, be their own boss, and decided that's what I wanted to do. I have never regretted that decision.

I thought a lot about the business name. Through the years, I had visited many dealers and was always most impressed with those that had the owner's name and brand name. So my dealership, shown below, became Wallem International, Inc.

The dealership maintained three IH franchises: farm equipment, trucks and light industrial. There were nine employees with the business I bought. All but one continued on after the change of ownership. With three franchises we needed to expand to be profitable, and I started interviewing prospective employees.

One area I was not prepared for was hiring mechanics. My jobs with Harvester had always been marketing oriented, and I had spent very little time in service departments. I lucked out here. The service manager who stayed on from the prior dealership was a master at his job. Ed O'Donnell spent his day on the shop floor training apprentices, overseeing jobs that were underway, and always complimenting good work when he saw it. (He drove the office manager nuts, though; the job tickets were always piled up and late getting to the office.) I quickly realized he should interview prospective mechanics after I did, and then we would decide together if we should hire the individual. That worked out well.

It became obvious that Ed was also our "closer." Customers would often look at a new machine with a salesman, then go out in the shop and ask our service manager if it was a good product. They trusted his judgment.

Our dealership was very fortunate to have an outstanding parts manager for most of the 17 years. Ron White supervised his department employees and a $500,000 inventory. It was a challenging job and he did it professionally.

Over the 17 years at the dealership, I look back with great pride at the really great people that operated the business in all the departments. Some are still friends these many years later.

During my first weeks, I realized how my past experiences were affecting my thoughts. As a kid, when we visited

A lot of farm equipment is sold on a pickup's hood. The author, far left, is shown with the Greenlees, who were great customers and friends beginning in 1969.

the dealership my dad went to, it was like going into a candy store. The tractor in the showroom smelled like new paint. Now I had a showroom. It still smelled like new paint!

Another observation of my years working for Harvester was that the most successful owners spent their time "out and about," not sitting at their desk. The best ones would touch base with parts, service and sales managers first thing each day, then get out in the community and farms to meet customers and get acquainted. As a new owner I found that effective.

As a teenager, I worked at an IH dealership, first as a mechanic's gofer, then as a salesman. It was an exciting place with trucks and farm equipment. Just driving a new L-185 semi-tractor from the yard into the shop made me feel like I was a trucker. After becoming a dealer, I felt that same excitement. Great feeling!

Another dealership trait I copied was keeping Wallem International neat and clean. We hired a janitor to maintain that appearance. One of the first additions was a flag pole. The Stars and Stripes went up every morning, came down at closing time.

HARVESTER SUCCESSES = DEALER PROFITABILITY

The '70s brought about some of Harvester's best new products. Every successful introduction not only boosted sales volume but had an instant effect on parts and service sales.

In 1971, we got a big boost in sales from the announcement of the 400 Cyclo planter. It was revolutionary in delivering seeds from the planter's hopper to the drill. While the U.S. Patent Office recognizes a couple of Minnesota farmers, Leo and Claude Loesch, as the 1972 patent holders, there's long been discussion about a 1956 invention by an Australian farmer named Albert Fuss and his Gyral air seeder.

The Gyral company, headquartered in Toowoomba, Queensland, lays claim to the concept, stating on its website: "We invented and patented the first pneumatic broadacre air seeder in the world and pioneered its early development. Albert Fuss set about making a seeder mechanism with central distribution." It was called the Gyral air seeder. The idea was to use compressed air and a rotating drum to select wheat seeds to be planted from a hopper and deliver them to the drill.

GYRAL - IT'S AUSTRALIAN FOR AIRSEEDER!

When Albert Fuss invented and patented the world's first broadacre airseeder in 1956, little did he realise that his invention would revolutionise crop planting world-wide.

Gyral and the Fuss family remain at the forefront of tillage and seeding equipment development, and manufacture a range of machinery designed to "get crops out of the ground".

Gyral's founder Albert Fuss and his prototype airseeder - Gyral held world-wide patents for pressurised bin airseeder technology.

The Loesches worked long and hard to make their air planter work for seeds of different sizes, such as corn and soybeans, by making drums with different sized holes. The abstract in the image below describes the function that earned the patent.

United States Patent
Loesch et al.

[15] 3,637,108
[45] Jan. 25, 1972

[54] **SEED PLANTER**

[72] Inventors: **Leo J. Loesch; Claude E. Loesch,** both of Kimball, Minn. 55353

[22] Filed: **June 25, 1969**

[21] Appl. No.: **836,480**

Related U.S. Application Data

[63] Continuation-in-part of Ser. No. 684,357, Nov. 20, 1967, abandoned, which is a continuation-in-part of Ser. No. 599,792, Dec. 7, 1966, abandoned.

[52] U.S. Cl....................**221/211,** 222/167, 222/194, 302/2

[51] Int. Cl..**B65g 15/02**

[58] Field of Search 221/211, 266, 167, 194; 294/64; 222/220, 221, 222, 223, 194, 167; 209/113, 86; 302/2

[56] **References Cited**

UNITED STATES PATENTS

1,997,791 4/1935 Hoberg et al. ....222/222 X
2,479,534 8/1949 Bergh et al........................222/221 X

FOREIGN PATENTS OR APPLICATIONS

802,899 10/1958 Great Britain........................221/211

Primary Examiner—Robert B. Reeves
Assistant Examiner—Francis J. Bartuska
Attorney—Williamson, Palmatier & Bains

[57] **ABSTRACT**

A seed dispenser for a planter including a drum with a shell at the periphery with openings in which seeds are held by positive air pressure within the drum, while moving air within the drum sweeps away all excess seeds from the openings, and seed discharge tubes receiving seeds from said openings and carrying the seeds out of the drum by the air under pressure in the drum.

International Harvester spent millions and endless man hours perfecting the Loesches' concept to create the Cyclo planter. It was an immediate success, and during the early '70s, we sold more than 20 each year. Our set-up shop was busy during the late winter months, preparing them for delivery. Training meetings were held to instruct buyers on proper operation of the game-changing planter.

The Cyclo air planter made history. The air monitoring system was accurate, reliable and relatively simple, making it easy for customers to understand. Once more, Harvester had revolutionized one of the primary tools on the farm.

Penner Auctions

SCOUT — ANOTHER WINNER FOR BOTH IH AND DEALERS

The International Scout was described in Chapter Ten as the precursor to the modern SUV. For us in the dealership, the Scout was a real winner. It provided year-round sales volume, and was like nothing else on the market. Look at the prices in the ad on the next page. Can you imagine a vehicle selling for less than $7,000 new when today's SUVs routinely exceed $40,000?

SUCCESSES AND FIRSTS

The 77's are here . . . .

The 76's are now at the lowest prices ever!
(The best of both worlds)
IH SCOUT MODELS . . . .

NEW	DEMO	DEMO
1976 Scout XLC	**1976 Scout Traveler**	**1976 Scout 4 x 4 XLC**
V8, automatic, power steering, radio, chrome wheels, buckets, roll bar, 10" tires, convertible top and hard top!	3000 miles, AM-FM radio, buckets, air, automatic, tilt wheel, radial tires.	3300 miles, buckets, automatic, radio, power steering, 2 speed transfer case, locking hubs, white spoke wheels, L10x15 RWL tires,
list $7480	list $7325	list $7182
NOW $6775	NOW $6275	NOW $6395

Wallem INTERNATIONAL, Inc.
PHONE 547-5359   Route 20 East   BELVIDERE, ILL.

Dealerships were dealt a double blow by Harvester when the International pickup line was discontinued in 1975, followed in 1980 by the cancellation of the Scout. Both were very successful products to represent, and were stable, year-round sellers that we relied on.

Fortunately, we were able to continue selling heavier trucks, and grain trucks were a huge part of our business. The rest of the mid-range International trucks were popular in our area, and provided one more source of sales volume year-round.

PRODUCT ANNOUNCEMENTS — A SOCIAL EVENT

Announcing new products created opportunities for us, and our customers, to have a lot of fun. We discovered that customers and their families really enjoyed a summer evening at our store. I'm sure the free food and entertainment didn't hurt!

One of our customers had a country music band, and if you look closely at the white truck with the flatbed in the above photo, you'll see the band playing to the crowd. The slight hillside at one side of our property, with hay bales lined up for seating, made a good grandstand.

CUB CADETS

Chapter Eight outlined the national success of the Cub Cadet. We found similar acceptance at our store. Belvidere is near Rockford, and the Cadet market in both was strong. We never fell below fifty units a year, often selling more.

Later, we opened a separate store in Machesney Park, pictured on the next page, Wallem Outdoor Power. Between Cub Cadets and Ski-Doo snowmobiles the store remained busy year-round. Service was a big part of the Cadet business, as most owners don't want to perform maintenance themselves.

MORE ABOUT TRACTOR PULLS

Early red tractor successes in pulling contests, thanks to superior IH engines, were part of Chapter Five. There's more to that story, and it involves my dealership.

Our parts department began selling turbo-chargers and other engine parts to a young entrepreneur in a Chicago suburb. His name was Jerry Lagod. Jerry had begun working for the International Harvester Engine Division in Melrose Park in 1962, fresh out of college with a mechanical engineering degree. He was a member of the team that developed the iconic DT466 in-line six.

In Jerry's introduction to the National Tractor Pullers Association Pulling Hall of Fame in 2013, his time at IH was described as follows:

> Jerry worked primarily with the 300 and 400 series engines for IH during his tenure. They were looking to phase out the 407 engine with the newer 414 and 436 versions. The IH tractor sales group was looking for something more powerful in the field, so marketing the new series of workhorse tractors of the day to the farmers was paramount. After many of these models sold,

bragging rights for agricultural power over your neighbors' began to really take off at tractor pulling contests at the county fairs. Much to the chagrin of the IH brass, farmers began complaining about the older 407 series engines "kicking ass" (as Lagod characterized it) at these contests over the newer, more powerful production counterparts. "The higher ups did not like this situation," Lagod said, "so the job was given to me to make the 436 engine outperform the 407 engine." From this new task grew additional research and development responsibilities for Jerry as the 1960s rolled into the '70s.

Even with his racing background, Jerry did not know what a tractor pull was – he had never seen one. Lagod thought that two tractors were chained back to back. After seeing the first one, he was hooked, and made a number of pulling contacts. Every puller seemed to want a part of Jerry's "IH power" touch. Lagod finished the project in IH's view, as the 436 project found power gains that the brass were looking for to satisfy the farming segment of their business. However, Lagod had so much more on the table to implement. He had an in-line pump package drafted, as well as the first water injection system diagrammed instead of the ice chest for the bulky intercoolers of the day. He could not convince the brass at IH to continue the project, as the liability of this was of major concern.

Lagod saw the large, untapped market in the sport of pulling, and decided to part ways with IH.

Jerry opened up his own engine shop in an old dairy barn behind his house. He named his company Hypermax Engineering. My memory of visiting his shop is that it was full of test equipment, engine heads and various parts.

After I sold the dealership, I lost touch with Jerry, but Ron White, who was parts manager at our store, told me years later that Hypermax had become much bigger and was the go-to supplier of turbochargers and other performance add-ons to the red tractor pulling crowd who were dominating tractor pulls. Now, more than 40 years later, Lagod and the Hypermax brand are still household names in tractor pulling. The company manufactures its own engine blocks, cylinder heads, turbochargers, injection pumps, connecting rods, intake manifolds, and various other competition-only parts.

Hypermax Engineering had much to do with IH tractors becoming dominant in tractor pulling. In later years, Jerry and his son built a dragster using the DT466 that produced over 3,000 horsepower, and set the world record for fastest diesel dragster at 216 mph in 6.69 seconds!

Hypermax's first customer, John D. Thompson of Marshall, Illinois, on "Bad Dog," an IH 1466 (Red Power Magazine)

A GODSEND FOR IH DEALERS

We covered the industry-changing impact of the Axial-Flow combine in Chapter Seven, but I wanted to mention its equally profound impact on IH dealers.

When it debuted at our dealership in 1979, the rotary-harvesting combine was such a game changer that we found it easy to sell. Twelve were sold early in that season and more later. It was a dream to demonstrate, easy to adjust and field loss was small. The separating capacity was well above the old 815 and 915 machines.

From the dealer's standpoint, no farm machine has more profit potential than a combine. All departments benefit: the sales department first because it can be the highest profit sale of all machines with its high selling price, then parts and service for future years. As an example, the corn head on combines has fast wearing parts and each season's parts sales are substantial. And with only a few weeks of use each year, it isn't uncommon for these machines to continue in service for 20 years or more.

Trade-in sales often create another source of profit for dealers. Of course, that depends on a proper and careful appraisal and making sure the allowance for the trade is right — and the farm economy doesn't go into a recession! As mentioned, 1979 Axial-Flow sales were great, but we had no way of knowing a decline in farm equipment purchases was coming. A combination of factors, including the Russian grain embargo and interest rates well into double digits were major causes, and the used combines we took in as trades stayed on the lot for a long time after that great 1979 year. Sitting outside in the elements is hard on a combine, and we had no room to store them inside. That story, however, goes beyond the scope of this book.

Our Axial-Flow buyers had only good comments about the machines. It was truly a star and it remains the rotary harvesting benchmark for the industry.

SUCCESSES AND FIRSTS

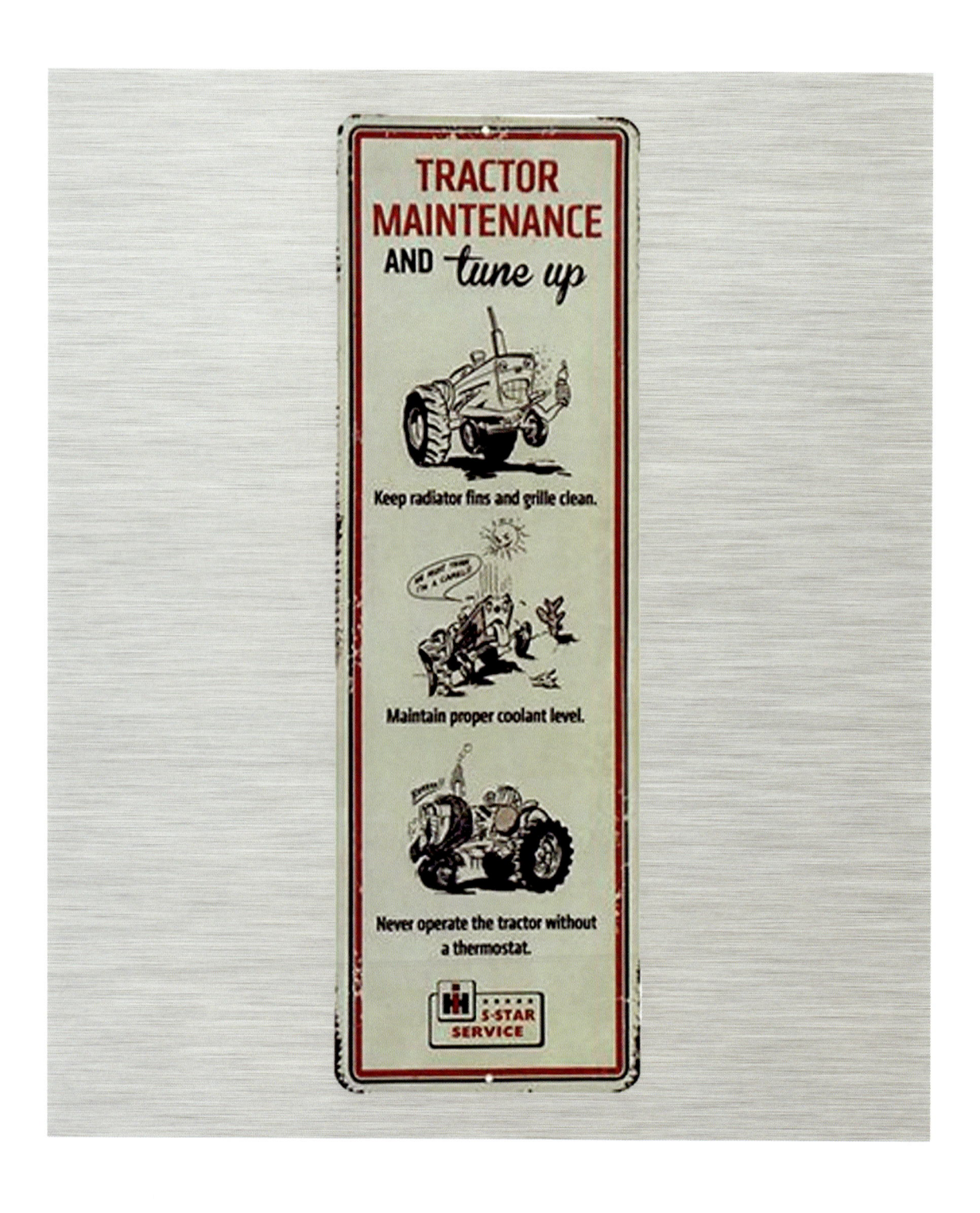

CHAPTER FIFTEEN

LEAVING THE IRON PUSHER IMAGE BEHIND

In 1975, Harvester announced a challenge to dealers to become an XL dealer — to make a commitment to "excel" in meeting customer service needs. Over half of the dealers committed early on, with more joining in as time went on. Yours truly, with a dealership in Belvidere, was the first to sign up in Illinois.

J.B. Schenck, who was in charge of the program for IH, described the program in *Implement and Tractor* magazine as a sophisticated approach to service "designed to meet today's sophisticated equipment."

Each dealer received a large bronze "XL Dealer" wall plaque to advise customers of the achievement. And it wasn't just a meaningless marketing gimmick. Dealers had to agree to meet certain standards, ranging from shop size to the size of their credit line, and invest time and money in computerized parts and accounting systems. I agreed with other dealers who said the XL program forced us to update our operations much faster than we probably would have otherwise, which was a benefit to the customer.

One of the significant stipulations of the program was a requirement for a plan of succession. This would provide customers with the assurances that the business would carry on in the event of the owner's demise.

A Davenport, Iowa, dealer, Dean Bassett, said the computerized parts system that was part of the XL program was essential in keeping track of over 9,000 parts and making sure he had them in stock when farmers needed them. The XL program was unique in the industry. It set a higher standard that progressive dealers could achieve.

an "XL Dealer"

The "XL Dealer" appointment is the highest honor we can bestow on an International Harvester Dealer.

It symbolizes a firm commitment to the highest Dealer standards of customer service.

It means adopting such advanced systems as data processing to assure you faster special parts delivery; a full line of IH parts and *above* average service facilities; knowledge and availability of the latest finance plans and systems to help you get the equipment you need, when you need it; and, above all, a desire to change and adapt to your changing needs.

INTERNATIONAL HARVESTER
QUAD CITY REGION
Davenport, Iowa 52808

IH support of the XL program included newspaper ads.

AUTHOR'S NOTE: Concurrently with the XL program for dealers, IH initiated a program for farm customers: Pro-Ag. Dale Simpson had a long career at IH: local, regional and then national responsibilities. I asked him to describe Pro-Ag, which he helped administer.

> In the early '70s, through various connections and relationships with Purdue University's Department of Agricultural Economics and Dr. D. Howard Doster, International Harvester set out on a path to develop and commercialize a "B-10" type model customized and developed specifically for IH. It was branded "Pro-Ag."

Why would IH do this?

IH was in the "iron" business, and had been for years. IH was a global company, selling tractors, combines, implements and repair parts, trucks and construction equipment; horizontally and vertically integrated.

Where is the "fit?"

Competition was fierce. Especially for those rapidly growing "super farmer" types that were expanding their operations and buying new and larger equipment they needed to farm larger acreages they were adding through purchase or rental, as well as clearing the tree lines and fences on existing fields. Something was needed to set them apart from other equipment manufacturers; something that could help the company and dealers alike attract and retain these new super farmers as customers and as partners into the future.

In a short time, the Pro-Ag program was birthed and rolled out to a few regions that covered the central Corn Belt states. Purdue grads who had working knowledge of the Purdue B-10 model were hired at IH world headquarters to train and shepherd this "computer thing" to and throughout the sales and marketing organization and dealer network.

In late 1975, Pro-Ag seminars were being held at regional offices, such as the Quad Cities (Iowa-Illinois) Region. Select IH Dealers would invite key customers to a two-day program to meet with Company management, listen to speakers about commodity markets and practices, and provide input/feedback to engineering about current and future equipment requirements.

But the focus and "center-piece" of the two-day event was a chance to "computer model" their farm and then run several "what-if" scenarios to see what impact to the bottom line occurred.

The "short version" of the process went as follows:

- *25 or so farmers complete a multi-page input form (paper with pencil) with assistance from the seminar leader and company trained assistants stepping the group through the process, providing one-on-one assistance.*
- *Each input form was then keyed into a terminal for processing by the huge IBM Mainframe located near Chicago.*
- *Large "green bar" printouts were waiting in the early hours the next*

morning for specialists to review. Often, there were keying errors or glitches that needed to be corrected and re-run if possible.
- *Meet with the growers again right after breakfast to review the results:*
   This is your farm today.
   The "shadow prices" show you where your operation is constrained, or you have opportunity for profitability by making changes to equipment size, labor, or crop mix.
- *Farmers prioritized and make a change (they were asked to consider things they want to look at in advance of attending the seminar).*
- *Changes were entered, re-run, and new printouts reviewed.*
- *"AH HA!" moments galore!*
- *"OK, let's try this!" Farmers are understanding and excited now.*
- *"WOW! This is GREAT!"*
- *"Time to go!"*
- *"Aw, shucks, I want to run some more scenarios!"*
- *"OK, one more."*
- *"Sorry, time to go."*
- *"How can I do more?" Please!*
- *"Talk to your dealer."*

As Pro-Ag seminars were completed and tremendous positive feedback came from the IH dealers and their community of customers, demand for seminars grew. Specialists were trained or hired at the Region level to focus on handling the growing demand and investigate ways to grow the availability.

That's where I came in. In May 1976, I was a recent graduate with a BS degree in finance, a newly hired IH sales management trainee cycling through various departments to learn about the organization. An Illinois farm boy, I had done computer business modeling and optimization similar to Pro-Ag in my college coursework.

Rob Boysen, Agri-Business Manager at the IH Quad Cities Region asked me to sit in on a Pro-Ag seminar as I was cycling through my management trainee program. After one day at that seminar and working with a few growers from Northern Illinois, I was hooked. I pulled an all-nighter fixing printouts so they would be available for the farmers first thing in the morning.

But I was excited: This "Pro-Ag thing" made total sense to me. Before long, I was sitting and working with several farmers helping them understand what the printout data meant and guiding them through various scenarios to test. This was a great way to try out different things on their farms to determine the sequence or order by profitability of the change. Mind you, this was in the early days of computers. No PCs, and certainly long before cell phones, email, internet or wi-fi. I still relied on my dog-eared copy of Doane's Facts and Figures for Farmers *as my go-to reference book!*

My sales management training program finished fairly soon after and I was assigned to the Pro-Ag team. I loved it. It fit me like a glove.

This first job assignment teamed me up with Rob Boysen and M.O. Stevenson, Rob's boss, to grow Pro-Ag in the Illinois/Iowa Region. And we made a great team.

M.O., our senior statesman, would oversee and run the traps with region management regarding direction and budgets, and with his guidance and endorsement we were granted pretty much what we requested to make the Pro-Ag program go and grow.

Looking back, I suspect M.O. had to fight several battles with other regional departments and district managers who were fighting for more people and budgets. But Pro-Ag had strong support at world HQ in Chicago, as well as with J. P. Hitchner, our regional manager.

It didn't take long before we came to the obvious conclusion that the seminar approach was too limited in market scope and could not accommodate the numbers of farmers wanting access to this technology. And it certainly did not meet the requirement of firmly connecting the IH dealers and their customers and prospects. We were only skimming the surface of farmer demand. But how do we make this available anytime a farmer wanted to "run his ideas through the computer?"

After lots of meetings with farmers who'd graduated Pro-Ag seminars, dealers and our HQ management group, the answer was pretty straightforward: figure out how to use the new computer technology available to our dealers for business management and parts systems to provide local access to farmers. And leverage Company specialists' efforts through trained dealer specialists.

I was assigned the task of developing and conducting a regional dealer *training program with assistance from our folks at HQ. Others were charged with finding technology to allow us to submit data remotely, from dealer business computer terminals, and others if possible. Using the U.S. Mail was not an option.*

Before long, we were taking our dealer training meetings on the road and arming folks at the dealerships to work directly with their customers. Soon, my first laptop arrived. Well, sort of — if you can call a Texas Instruments "dumb" terminal with two round, rubber acoustic couplers on the top a laptop! It required the handset from a telephone be inserted after dialing up the IH computer center to gain access to a carrier signal so I could key in the data to the mainframe and receive printouts on its slow-speed thermal printer. I can still hear the printers buzzing back and forth printing reports in the small hours of the night while I tried to sleep!

My evenings in small town motels often included advising the front desk person not to check my phone line because it would be tied up for hours sending and receiving data. Remember, this was long before most motels had computers. More than once after entering data for a half-hour I would hear the carrier signal drop, and as I picked up the phone handset off its couplers, I would hear "Hello. This is the front desk. We were wondering what was going on 'cause we saw your light on an awful long time and heard these funny sounds..."

Ugh! Luckily, my access time scheduled on the mainframe computer had not expired. (Can you imagine having to schedule access to a computer? Typically, my schedule was from 11p.m. to 2 a.m.)

Unfortunately, all the data was lost, or the printout job cancelled, so I was forced to start over. Hours wasted, but it was still a new dawn for computer technology in the agricultural sector.

Many dealers were successfully trained across several regions and it did prove to bring customers and dealers into a closer partnership or advisory relationship.

Pro-Ag also resulted in equipment sales. Many growers did not understand their serious bottlenecks at planting time had a huge negative economic impact on their operation, and limited their ability to add additional acres profitably. Once they saw the opportunity cost in black and white, they could begin to make the needed changes with support from their partners and bankers.

Pro-Ag also helped farmers, their wives and lenders understand the value of adding part-time or full-time labor to their operation which would free up the farmer to spend more time on planning, marketing or other management matters that improved profitability.

It allowed them to "Test, before you Invest." It brought modern management techniques to the farm office or kitchen table.

Ag lenders loved Pro-Ag. They saw and understood the value that it brought to their lending decisions and the profitability of their clients who were growing into unknown territory. Pro-Ag helped to provide a road map and sequencing of purchase decisions over multiple seasons. It introduced strategic planning to the farmer's toolbox. It supported risk management and marketing plans as crop mixes were evaluated. And so much more.

Being a part of the "Pro-Ag" team opened doors to me that I doubt I would ever have passed through:

- *As a young manager, I was able to meet and present to IH executives my Pro-Ag experiences, and they asked me for my input and recommendations;*
- *I was able to represent IH at an American Society of Association Executives meeting in San Antonio and present how IH was taking Pro-Ag to the marketplace;*
- *I connected with numerous top-flight, innovative and forward thinking IH dealer principals and their teams. I'm still friends with many today;*
- *But most of all, the many, many farmers I met and befriended during those several years, over a meal, or coffee and fresh home-baked pastries with their business plans and details spread out around us was such an incredible blessing and an honor.*

To this day, the things I learned in Pro-Ag are still applicable, and I find myself referring to them on a regular basis.

IH is gone. And the computer reels for an IBM mainframe containing the Pro-Ag programming code is likely sitting in a dusty archive somewhere, or long discarded, relegated to the trash heap of merger history.

That said, Pro-Ag can and always will be counted as a success of the International Harvester Company.

Pro-Ag: It all Adds Up!

The "Pro-Ag" initiative included a 1976 limited edition Bulova watch for participants. The white card in lower center reads: "In commemoration of the historical introduction of the Pro-Ag Line, IH has authorized the issuance of a limited number of specially imprinted timepieces. Wear this daily as a reminder of our commitment to serve our customer, better than anyone in the industry. It is time to lead and time to excel … the time is now!"

Photos by www.watchadoption.com.au

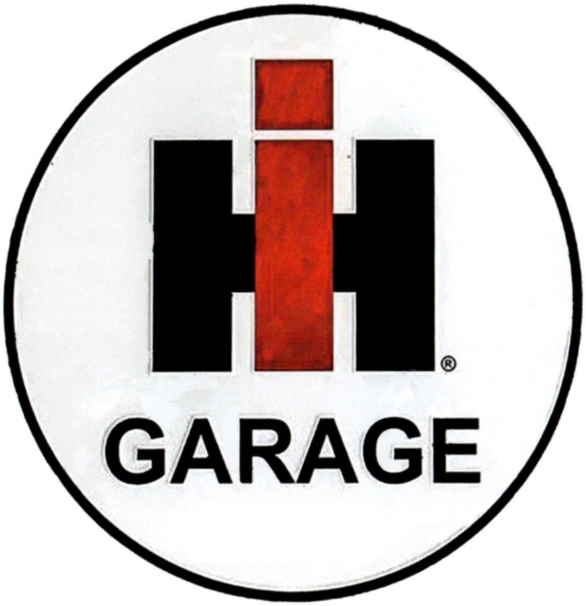
GARAGE

At its peak, International Harvester had Works, subsidiaries, branch subsidiaries and representatives in over 60 countries.

CHAPTER SIXTEEN

INTERNATIONAL HARVESTER FOREIGN OPERATIONS

International Harvester certainly lived up to its name with an aggressive effort to market equipment overseas. The effort to become "international" began in the late 1800s when the McCormick Company signed up distributors throughout the world to sell reapers. By the early 1900s, manufacturing and sales locations were firmly in place worldwide.

International Harvester Export Company contracted with independent contractors outside the U.S. In the mid-1960s, the Export Company had 118 distributors in over 70 countries. Some had only farm equipment contracts, some had multiple lines including motor truck and construction equipment.

The Export Company maintained four offices across the globe: Latin America, with headquarters in Lima, Peru; Africa and the Middle East, based in Beirut; Europe, with offices in Brussels; and Pacific, based in Singapore.

Some of these men had responsibility for distributors in several countries, and could speak more than one language. I traveled with many of them, and one of our representatives was conversant in nine languages.

Entirely separate entities were the subsidiary companies in major markets. They were separate companies wholly owned by International Harvester. Listed below are those operating in 1966, just in the European theatre, as an example.

> International Harvester Co. of Belgium, S.A.
> Denmark – A/S International Harvester Co.
> International Harvester France
> Germany – International Harvester Co., mbH
> International Harvester Company of Great Britain, Ltd.
> Spain – International Harvester de Espana S.A.
> Sweden – AB International Harvester Company
> Switzerland – International Harvester Company A.G.

Many other subsidiaries were on different continents.

Changes occurred in these companies many times throughout the decades, including the CaseIH formation in 1984. Some had manufacturing plants, some did not. Even though many IH products from U.S. plants were sold by the subsidiaries, some of their plants also produced successful tractors, trucks and implements that better fit their local markets. They would sell their production through the Export Company to other countries as well.

I spent two years (1966-68) as Manager of Farm Equipment Export Sales. Travel took me to 52 countries. Recently, I have been asked about the extent of foreign activity by International Harvester, and I'm happy to relive those memories.

TWO YEARS OF WORLDWIDE TRAVEL FOR IH
1966-1968

It was a time when air travel did not involve cell phones, laptops, tablets or the TSA. Suitcases didn't even have wheels yet! Knowing what we do today, it's shocking to think airlines allowed cigarettes, pipes and cigars; no restrictions.

In my 2019 IH book *The Breakup,* I discussed the business side of my job with International Harvester during the years I was export manager. Here, I'll express my personal thoughts about some of those trips, and experiences that most people never have.

Some trips were a week, some were over four weeks. Shown below is the flight log involving one very long trip, beginning with a meeting in Lima, Peru, and ending in Tokyo.

> Sept. 30 Chicago to Miami, then on to Lima, Peru
> Oct. 7-9 Lima to Miami, on to L.A., overnight to Honolulu, on to Tokyo.
> Oct. 13 Hokkaido, Japan
> Oct. 16 Back to Tokyo, then to Taipei, Taiwan
> Oct. 22 Taipei to Singapore
> Oct. 28 Singapore to Tokyo
> Oct. 29 Tokyo to Chicago

The Lima-Miami-L.A.-Honolulu-Tokyo trip was a challenge. I changed planes in Miami, changed planes in L.A., and then flew to Honolulu for an overnight stay. Then on to Tokyo the next morning. Total number of hours in the air between Lima and Tokyo was 31. The fact that we flew first class helped greatly. More leg room, much better seats and great meals.

In 1966, I was one of the few Americans traveling there, and at 6'1," I guess you could say I "stood out in a crowd."

Komatsu, an IH partner, featured tractors on the roofs of their locations. From Tokyo to their HQ in Sapporo, the 1967 train traveled at 120 mph.

Hokkaido

A side trip to Hokkaido, the northernmost island in Japan, was full of surprises. As I boarded the plane in Tokyo, I noticed I was the only Caucasian on the flight. Prior to takeoff, the stewardess spoke on the microphone and welcomed me in English! Then she proceeded to talk to everyone else in Japanese. What a courtesy that was. Another surprise was the very small bed in the hotel in Hokkaido. Since virtually all its guests were Japanese, and there was no need for big beds!

Taiwan

The next stop was Taipei, Taiwan. As we flew over Vietnam that day, our captain announced that the Tet Offensive was underway. The war between U.S. troops and the Viet Cong was raging. I looked down from 30,000 feet at the wet marshland and felt for the U.S. soldiers down there, fighting in impossible conditions.

As I turned on the radio in my room that afternoon, I was shocked to hear that Major Don Holleder had been killed in action that morning in Vietnam. Don was named an All-American while playing football for West Point. In 1957, I was a novice tackle on the Hawaiian 25th Infantry Division team and Don was a teammate. He spent time showing me how to be a better player. All those years later, I sat in that hotel room thinking about Don.

That evening, our British representative volunteered to order a delicacy for me at dinner. Fried chicken feet in barbecue sauce. All I could think of was our chicken yard on the farm when I was a kid. I remembered what they stepped in, and it wasn't barbecue sauce. Suddenly, I wasn't hungry.

THE DARK CONTINENT

Africa has been called the dark continent since the 19th century, supposedly because the interior has always been considered dangerous and mysterious. My travels with IH took me throughout Africa, from one end to the other. It is larger than the U.S., China and Brazil combined, occupies 20% of the earth's surface, and is home to at least 55 different languages.

Tunisia

My first trip there started on a flight from Paris to Tunis, the capital of Tunisia. It is the northernmost country in Africa, bounded on the north and east by the Mediterranean Sea. A small country by North African standards, it is sandwiched between the much larger countries of Algeria to the west and Libya to the southeast.

I checked into the hotel late. Just before dawn, I was awakened by sounds of chanting. I looked out and saw an image that has stayed with me all these years: hundreds of workers walking to work, some singing and others talking. They all wore white from head to toe. The hotel was surrounded by olive groves and the men were finding their way through the trees.

Back in the '60s, Tunisia's biggest crop was olives, and olive oil remains its number one export. At that time, cotton was also a major crop, and my time there involved a contract for IH cotton pickers.

This particular trip was five weeks, and I carried just one suitcase. Dectoline shirts, made by Arrow, were popular then, especially for travel. They could be washed in the hotel room and dried overnight wrinkle-free. I only carried three, all white, because in those days we wore suits and ties all the time.

Libya

From Tunis, I flew the 480 miles to Tripoli, Libya, right on the Mediterranean. I best remember the engraved and carved jewel box that was in the shop next to the hotel. He wanted $35. I stopped back several times during the two days I was there, and he came down to $20. The day I left, I showed him my airline ticket, he could see I was leaving. I offered him $2 and he took it. It was one of my wife's favorite gifts from those travels. She still has it.

A flight to Sudan came next. It was 1,200 miles southeast, deeper into the heart of the African continent. The Russians had sold them cotton pickers but couldn't provide spare parts. Most of the machines had broken down the first year, and IH, in partnership with the Agency for International Development (AID), had agreed to provide IH pickers. That's why I was there. The memorable part of the trip was departure time. It was the height of summer temperatures, and the air was too thin for a normal departure time. We left at 3 a.m. The density altitude at that time of night provided a safe takeoff.

Just before the takeoff, I was in a left side window seat, and was watching the baggage handler load suitcases on the conveyor into the plane. One suitcase was halfway up when it fell off and broke open. The handler stuffed everything back in, closed it and loaded it back on the conveyor. The suitcase had red tape wrapped around the handle. It was a grey Samsonite. It was mine!

Kenya

IH had a subsidiary office in Nairobi, which was my next stop on this trip, and was another 1,200 mile flight, south-southeast from Khartoum. Nairobi is at a higher elevation than Denver. At almost 6,000 feet, it takes a day to become accustomed to the thinner air. It was also strange to see no screens in the windows, as insects at this elevation were almost non-existent.

A vivid memory comes back to me about visiting a wildlife refuge. We were in an enclosed Jeep and found ourselves only about 25 yards from two sleeping lions. Our guide made it very clear that we were to stay in the vehicle. He indicated that the animals can wake up and attack anything they think is a threat. So we stayed inside!

Nigeria

From Kenya, I flew to Nigeria, about a five-hour flight. IH had long maintained a corporate membership with the Agency for International Development (AID), which is part of the Food and Agricultural Organization (FAO) of the United Nations. My responsibilities on this job included representing IH and making contact with the AID offices during my travels. That was my reason for the trip to Nigeria.

As I got off the plane in Lagos, a shocking sight faced me. Hundreds of little kids surrounded the stairs off the plane, begging. Many were malnourished. I'll never forget the sight. It was the saddest experience during all my years of IH travel, and I suspect conditions haven't changed much. At the time of my visit, the population was 55 million. In 2020, it was estimated to be 206 million.

I stayed overnight in the town of Ibadan, where the Nigerian AID office was located. I witnessed cattle being butchered right in the street, in the hot sun. I avoided meat at dinner that evening.

Back in Lagos the next day, I met with the Nigerian Secretary of Agriculture.

He had been educated in the U.S. and then returned to his home country and worked his way up to this job. I asked what his goals for the future were. He wanted to get a job in a more modern country!

Oil has been the major source of revenue for Nigeria.

Ivory Coast

Straight west of Lagos about 1,000 miles, this was the last African stop scheduled for this trip. A French-speaking nation, Ivory Coast, officially the Republic of Côte d'Ivoire, had declared independence from France just six years before my visit there.

IH had shipped a Model 105 combine for a demonstration in their rice harvest. It was done in collaboration with AID, and I represented IH in that demonstration. I'm mentioning it here because I saw workers who were seeing a machine do the job that they had been doing for a lifetime. They jumped up and down, shouted and pointed. They were well aware that this machine might replace their back-breaking efforts doing the same job. Photos are on the next pages.

I still remember thinking that they were responding in a manner similar to how farmers in the U.S. may have in the 1800s when they witnessed Cyrus McCormick first demonstrating his reaper.

Paris

If I recall correctly, when I boarded the Air Afrique flight in Abidjan for the trip from the Ivory Coast to Paris, we were told to expect a flight time of more than nine hours. (Imagine a flight from New York to Los Angeles and back without stopping.)

What they didn't say is it would be over the Sahara desert most of the time. It was a clear day, as it usually is over the desert, and I looked out every once in awhile. Nothing but sand, hour after hour. Very little vegetation appeared, but we were at least 30,000 feet up. It was really hard to believe that there is that much desert anywhere.

Demonstrating the Model 105 rice combine in the Ivory Coast

In those years, airline dining really was fine dining — in first class, at least. Air Afrique featured a nine-course French dinner, with such dishes as *Pirogue de foie gras en gelee*, and *Darne de capitaine de l'ebrie*, accompanied by champagne, cognac and liqueurs. All that food probably helped pass the time.

Chicago

After a short meeting in Paris the next morning, I was en route home, a short flight in comparison with the prior day. The best part of these trips was always seeing my family again. Back in those days, they could meet me at the gate as I departed the plane. After being gone five weeks, it was a wonderful greeting.

SUCCESSES AND FIRSTS   133

The Model 105 combine takes on an Ivory Coast rice paddy.

MIDDLE EAST AND SOUTH AMERICA

This trip brought some unexpected experiences. The first leg was a three-country trip, all located on the Mediterranean Sea. First stop was Beirut, Lebanon, a beautiful city in those days where we maintained an export office for representatives overseeing that part of the world. The domestic U.S. farm equipment division had encouraged a very competent product specialist, Jay Suchland, to join us in the export division. As his supervisor, it was necessary for me to accompany him to Damascus, Syria, for a work permit in that country.

I'll always remember that trip to Damascus. As we drove up from Beirut, the desert reminded me of biblical times. Scattered nomad tents and flocks of sheep dotted the hillsides. Some things never change. This area was known as home of the Phoenicians, all the way back to 300 BC.

The cab driver we hired for the trip insisted on buying our lunch. He bought lamb sandwiches on the street in Damascus, on a very hot day. That night, after I had returned to Beirut and flown to the Mediterranean island of Cyprus, I woke up at midnight with terrific stomach pains.

I expected food poisoning from the noon sandwich, which had tasted rancid. We always carried charcoal pills for this purpose, and after several hours I was OK. I was fortunate, because this was the only digestive problem I had with food during two years of overseas travel.

The next stop was Caracas, Venezuela, but to get there I had to fly to Madrid to catch the long flight over the Atlantic to Venezuela. We got into Caracas at five a.m., spent two days there for a meeting with distributors, and then I was glad to return home to Chicago.

Europe

This job involved numerous trips to Europe and my flight schedule would often appear challenging, if not crazy. For example, leaving Chicago's O'Hare airport on January 13th, I arrived in London on the 14th, then on to Vienna and Belgrade for a week. On the 21st, it was a flight to Copenhagen, then three days later it was on to Oslo, and two days later a flight from Oslo to Kristiansand, and the next day to Amsterdam, and then Brussels. On February 1st, I landed in London, then on to Paris three days later, and three days after that to Lisbon, and on February 9, left Lisbon for New York, where I changed planes and flew to Chicago. Phew!

On January 14, 1968, I flew to Vienna to begin a road trip behind the Iron Curtain. At the time, official relations between the U.S. and the Soviet Bloc were icy as the Cold War hadn't yet thawed. Our representative for IH in those countries lived in Vienna. A remarkable man, he spoke nine languages and knew Eastern Europe well. I was excited to meet him in Vienna, known for so many things from architecture to its rich music and art history. I stayed in a living reminder of the city's majestic age, the beautiful Grand Hotel Wein. It was so much like I've always pictured a hotel in the home of Johann Strauss and many other composers, to look. A small group of violinists performed in the lobby playing waltzes. The atmosphere was magical.

The Grand Hotel Wein, Vienna, Austria

The next morning, we drove into Yugoslavia and on to Belgrade. While Vienna and the Austrian countryside were colorful and appeared prosperous, a lack of prosperity greeted us as we crossed the border. Buildings weren't as well-maintained.

Our purpose in going to Belgrade was to visit a 20,000 acre state farm that had just purchased 20 IH Cyclo-planters. We were invited to a banquet to celebrate the new relationship between IH and the state farm. During the speeches the farm manager announced to the audience that he had a gift for me, a Communist Party membership card, and he was going to pay the $40 membership fee for me!

I struggled with the right words to reject his gift but told him that I appreciated his generosity. He stood up, laughed and said he wondered how I was going to avoid accepting it.

SOUTH AND CENTRAL AMERICA

IH did a great deal of business in this part of the world and my most frequent trips were to this part of the Southern Hemisphere.

Columbia

I'll never forget my trips to Bogota and Medellin. The first night I spent in Bogota, I was awakened about midnight with constant gunfire somewhere outside. When I asked the desk clerk about it the next morning, I was told it was a common sound in the neighborhood. On the next trip, I stayed in a different hotel. Same noises. I realized it's a common sound at night citywide.

Fast forward to a conversation I had in 2019 with my nephew who travels for Chevron. He told me about a trip to Bogota and the gunfire he heard overnight. Some things don't change!

The approach to the airport at Medellin parallels a mountain wall, which is quite close to the ILS (instrument landing system) path. Looking out the window on the left side, that mountain wall seemed incredibly close. Years later, that memory resurfaced when I read of the 2016 crash on that same approach, where 71 died.

Panama

We chose a farm near the Panama Canal for a product announcement. Our distributors from throughout South and Central America attended. Because six different languages were represented, we gave each guest a transistor radio tuned to his language. He then listened on his ear plugs to an interpreter backstage.

We arranged a tour of the Panama Canal for everyone. What a fantastic experience that was! We stood alongside the locks as the ships came through, and could hardly imagine how the canal got built so many years before, with 5,600 deaths from disease and accidents. It's truly a marvel of engineering and had IH built it, it would certainly be featured in this book.

I was back in Panama again in April 1967 when I heard on the hotel radio that a tornado in Belvidere, Illinois, had killed 24. That was only 40 miles from our home in Mount Prospect. What a scare that was! I was able to get through by phone to my wife and found that my family and our community was safe.

Out of frame is a Cub Cadet used to tow the bananas in Panama.

The Equator

Crossing the Equator for the first time used to be a big deal on some airlines. My first crossing was on August 20, 1966 on Air France, and they asked for a show of hands before takeoff. Several of us indicated it was our maiden voyage.

As we crossed the line, the cabin attendants gathered at each first-timer's seat and presented a certificate and a glass of champagne. My certificate is shown below.

Pan American was the first choice at IH for global travel. Pan Am Flight 001 flew around the world westbound, originating in San Francisco. A passenger could stay on this flight and circumnavigate the world. Pan Am Flight 002 originated in New York and traveled eastbound to the same cities. I don't recall how many times I rode on these two flights, but it was often.

Other carriers were used for different locations or times, with outstanding service on some, such as Air France, Air Afrique and JAL.

We avoided much of jet lag fatigue by following the advice of our company doctor. He recommended always resetting our watch to local time wherever we were, and eat, sleep, etc. on the same schedule we did at home. That worked well for me.

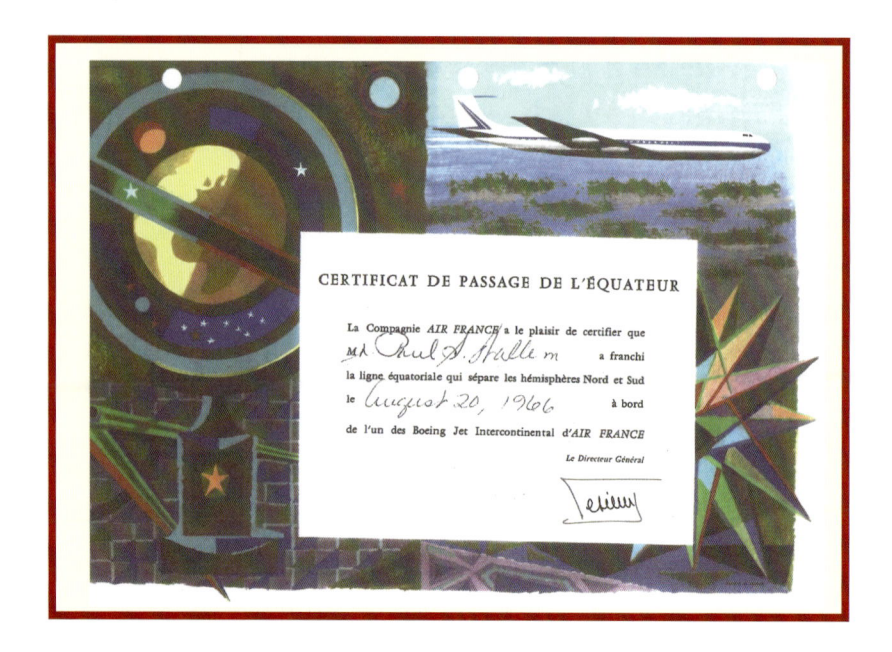

Visas and Shots

The IH travel department required details of my trips two weeks before departure. It would then request the visas needed for each country. If vaccinations were required they would advise our medical staff, who would call us in for the shots.

Communication

There's a whole generation — maybe two — to whom the concept of paying extra to dial long distance is foreign. But long distance phone calls in the '60s were extremely expensive. Even on a four-to-five week trip, I would call home only once. I did write home at least twice a week, describing to the kids and Joan where I was and what the countries were like. All business communication during the trips was by cable, which was similar to a telegram.

In conclusion, I feel fortunate my job at Harvester provided me the opportunity to travel so extensively in a relatively short period of time, I can assure you, though, it is not as glamorous nor exotic as it may seem. I was glad to do it, and I was glad when it ended.

MIDDLE EAST STORY

The Export Company office for the Middle East was in Beirut, Lebanon. The following account of that experience was submitted by Jay Suchland, who did a great job for us in that office after beginning his IH career in St. Louis. His long tenure with Harvester after Beirut included posts in Latin America and with CaseIH at Racine. He is retired and lives in Oro Valley, Arizona.

In April of 1966 I arrived in Beirut, Lebanon to take up my new position as Agricultural Equipment Representative covering Africa and the Middle East for the International Harvester Export Company. The IH Export

Company was tasked with managing the parent company's business interests in all countries of the world where there were no company owned affiliate companies. This was accomplished by locating, contracting and overseeing distributors for each of the main product lines, trucks, construction equipment and agricultural equipment, in each country where there was adequate sales potential and where IH did not have a subsidiary company.

Shortly after arriving in Beirut I was asked to travel to Greece to join others from the company to introduce mechanical cotton harvesting. The mechanical cotton harvester is a complex machine necessitating that the cotton fields and the plant itself must be prepared and managed in a particular way for mechanical harvesting to be effectively accomplished. Furthermore additional equipment must be added in the gins to efficiently gin cotton harvested mechanically rather than by hand. So the task of introducing mechanical harvesting would require convincing Greece government officials of the need to alter cotton farming practices and to spend the money required to update the gins. After that the task would be to train Ministry of Agriculture field agents and selected farmers to help prepare the way for successful mechanical harvesting.

We were fortunate in Greece to have a professional and effective distributor, Hellagricol. This company was very ably managed by Madam Poppy Soroglu. The service manager was Mimi Trepas who would be instrumental in training his servicemen, and farmers as well, to properly service the IH cotton pickers. Hellagricol was well acquainted in the Ministry of Agriculture and had set the table, so to speak, for our IH team to begin the task of first convincing and then training their key personnel. We spent some five or six weeks in total showing films and training materials to various groups in Athens and all over the cotton growing areas of Greece. One of our team members, John Bell, had prepared a binder titled: "Growing and Harvesting Cotton". The binder consisted of 16 labeled sections covering everything from the history of cotton, to cotton types, seed bed preparation, planting, caring for and harvesting. The *information and materials in the binder were used as a general guide for our presentations and later for training purposes. We had also assembled a very good set of films and visual aids to support our efforts. One 16 mm film was particularly useful in visually depicting the internal working mechanisms of our cotton picker.*

The IH cotton picker model we promoted for Greece, as an introductory machine, was the McCormick International Model 502 one-row picker. This unit was chosen rather than a self-propelled machine because it was more economical, and could be mounted on IH tractors already working in Greece. Even older used tractors could be utilized. To accomplish this, the tractor's transmission was modified so that the forward and reverse gears were reversed and the steering, clutch, brake and other controls were modified so that the machine could be conveniently operated with the operator facing towards what previously had been the rear of the tractor and was now the front of the cotton picker.

Our efforts paid off and Hellagricol was granted permission to import the first units. The other IH personnel went back to the States. I made several trips to Greece leading up to harvest time. Since cotton planting had already begun by the time the import permit was given there was little that could be done to influence the planting cycle. Luckily, the row spacing used was about 40 inches which was the spacing our pickers were designed for at that time. One critical field condition needed for the mechanical picker to work effectively was that the middle of the row needed to be as smooth as possible so that the picker drum vertical motion was limited as much as possible. This was a difficult parameter to accomplish given the existing irrigation and cultivating practices. The next new practice that needed to be introduced was defoliation as it was necessary to achieve as much leaf drop as possible prior to harvest to avoid having either leaf material mixed in, or having green stains on the cotton fibers from green leaf juices.

As harvest time approached we called for John Douglas to return from the Memphis factory, where IH pickers were manufactured, to operate the picker for our harvesting demonstration. John's expert operation during the demonstration was a huge factor in our success with picker sales for years to come. Of course, all the presentations and training contributed greatly, too, but it was John's skill in understanding and operating the mechanical picker that set us apart from Deere. Deere's office for managing Greece and the Middle East was in Western Germany. The people they sent to demonstrate their machine probably had never operated a picker before so the contrast in performance was striking. There was another competitor in Greece. The U.S.S.R. had entered into a barter arrangement with Greece to exchange their picker for Greek tobacco. The Soviet picker was based on the Rusk design which consisted of longer spindles that were friction driven rather than mechanically powered as with IH and Deere pickers. The demonstration of the Soviet machine went poorly. So poorly, tragically, that the owner of the Soviet picker committed suicide following the dismal performance of his machine. I was told that he was a devoted communist and was thoroughly embarrassed by the failure of the Soviet machine.

The net results of the efforts of our IH team, supported by Madam Soroglu and Hellagricol and with the professional skills of John Douglas, IH achieved complete dominance in picker sales in Greece for the next five years.

Off and on, during my five-plus years stationed in Beirut, I also tried to convince the Turkish authorities to allow the import of mechanical cotton pickers. They did finally permit the import of one machine for demonstration purposes, but refused to allow the machines to be sold. This was mostly because the indigenous population of Kurds provided the labor to hand pick cotton which was their main cash income for the year.

Jay Suchland

Jay recalls this photo was taken at the IH JV truck plant in Izmir, Turkey. "The No. 502 picker is the same model we sold in Greece and it's mounted on an IH tractor, possibly the B614, which was produced in Donncaster. The person kneeling in center front row is Rene Salameh who managed IH interests in Greece and Turkey. The others are all from our Turkish partner."

144 　IH　SUCCESSES AND FIRSTS

CHAPTER SEVENTEEN

HARVESTER FARM — BRINGING THE FARM TO THE CITY

The Museum of Science and Industry in Chicago — one of the largest science museums in the world—is home to more than 400,000 square feet of hands-on exhibits designed to spark scientific inquiry and creativity.

Opened during 1933's Century of Progress in a building from 1893's Columbian Exposition, MSI is the place where generations have been coming to see a wide variety of exhibits, including a full-size replica of a coal mine, a captured WWII German submarine, and a farm and farm equipment at Harvester Farm.

On July 3, 1946, Harvester opened its farm exhibit. The Harvester Farm presented a replica of a typical 160-acre farm, fully mechanized.

Thousands visited the Harvester Farm during the years it was open. It was an outstanding success in promoting U.S. agriculture and food production.

SUCCESSES AND FIRSTS			147

Lifelike farm animals and farm sound effects gave city kids (and adults) an idea of what rural America was like on the farm.

PAQUETTE'S
HISTORICAL FARMALL MUSEUM

FREQUENT GUEST QUESTIONS
Paquette's Historical Farmall Museum
Leesburg, Florida

AUTHOR'S NOTE: Stewart Paquette has assembled a remarkable and comprehensive collection of over 150 Farmall tractors and IH trucks dating back to 1923. Luckily for IH fans, he created a museum near Leesburg, Florida, where his carefully restored tractors are on display. What follows are frequently asked questions by guests at the Paquette Museum. The answers are the opinion of the author.

1. Is the McCormick name associated with the spice company?

I have been unable to locate any connection.

2. What is the best tractor ever built by IH?

A Farmall H owner would say his is the best of all time because more of that model were sold than any other tractor in history. A vintage 1206 owner will claim his tractor is best because its restored value is the highest of all older red tractors. So, I believe that the answer to your question lies in the eye of the beholder.

3. Why did IH go out of business?

There are many opinions on record regarding the IH dissolution. Some of the most obvious reasons appear to be:

Shareholder dividends paid for too many years at too high a rate. These funds were needed for plant modernization, field testing of new products, and keeping borrowing down. When Brooks McCormick was elected President in 1971 dividends were cut for the first time since 1939.

Large sums were committed to creating the Construction Equipment Division starting in 1945, as Caterpillar continued to dominate that market and control pricing.

Profits declined by 50% between 1966 and 1971. Corporate debt doubled in those years, in the face of increasing interest rates.

Timing of a "Perfect Storm" following many years of heavy borrowing. A very expensive strike in late 1979 and early 1980, at the same time as the Carter grain embargo reduced farm equipment demand. These events occurred at the same time as historically high interest rates hit and loss of the Company's borrowing power.

The good news is: Thirty seven years after CaseIH entered the picture, more red equipment than ever before carries the IH logo. International trucks now are worldwide as a result of VW/Traton. The traditional products of International Harvester — trucks and farm equipment — live on!

4. Was the Deering name involved or connected with the John Deere Tractor Co.?

There is no apparent historical connection between Deering Harvesting Co. (which merged with McCormick Harvesting Machine Co.) and John Deere. Discussions in 1909 between the IH president and the president of John Deere centered around each providing the other with products for dealers. Nothing came from the discussions.

5. What does Axial-Flow mean?

The definition of axial is "of or related to an axis." Another definition is "around an axis." Axial-Flow as it pertains to IH combines is its system of grain separation, i.e. a circular rotor inside a tube.

6. Why are some tractors painted yellow?

Yellow as it relates to IH tractors was the color of their light industrial equipment.

7. What did the reaper do?

The reaper sharply reduced the amount of labor required to harvest grain.

8. Why do you have refrigerators in the Museum?

Fowler McCormick's expansion plan in 1945 included purchase of an Evansville plant to produce freezer chests. Later refrigerators, air conditioners and dehumidifiers were added. The IH refrigerators and freezers were well built, but insufficient marketing resulted in the 1955 sale of the refrigeration line to Whirlpool.

9. What is a Torque Amplifier?

A Torque Amplifier reduced the tractor speed in each of the five gears, giving the tractor 10 speeds. It consisted of a precision planetary gear unit that gave a shift-free choice. By pulling one lever the TA reduced speed without clutching and shifting to a lower gear. Earliest use was in Super M-TAs, and 26,924 were sold with TAs. It continued to be offered in many models through the years.

10. Why are some tractors painted white?

Occasional IH promotions during the fifties involved white demonstrators to attract attention and draw prospects into the dealerships. The models involved were Cub, Farmall C, Farmall Super C and 37 baler.

11. When did IH start building trucks?

1907.

12. What does the word combine mean?

A combine performs four separate harvesting operations — reaping, threshing, gathering and winnowing — into a single process. Hence the word "combine."

13. What is a live PTO?

Live PTO (Power Take Off) allows the PTO to continue to operate even when the clutch that drives the tractor's transmission is disengaged.

14. What is the Farmall Regular tractor?

The original Farmall became known as the Regular. It was never officially known by that name, but it was commonly called that by farmers.

15. Are binders still being used?

Binders are still appearing in vintage farm shows. I do not know if any are in use in other parts of the world.

16. What is the three-point hitch and quick-change hitch?

Three-point hitch is the industry standard for attaching implement to tractor. IH featured a two-point hitch for a number of years that was called fast-hitch or quick-change hitch.

17. Why are some tractors raised up so high?

High-clear tractors are used to cultivate high-growing crops without damaging them.

18. Why does the Farmall A have an engine offset to one side?

The Farmall A, B and Cub tractors had engine offset design for unobstructed vision forward, especially for cultivating. Small farms everywhere still use the letter series tractors in daily operations.

19. Why do the early letter series have the name "McCormick Deering" painted above the Farmall name and later tractor series just have the name McCormick?

As the Farmall name came into wider use, some models had McCormick Deering in small letters. Through the '30s, the name Farmall became more prominent. Some of the implements used the McCormick decal only. By the '50s, the words McCormick and Deering were phased out.

20. Where is Navistar International corporate headquarters located?

Lisle, Illinois.

21. What is the Scout?

The Scout was a pre-SUV built by IH 1961 - 1980.

22. Is the museum owned by Navistar or CaseIH?

The museum is privately owned.

23. What is a tractor pull?

A tractor pull is a competitive event that matches tractors against each other in an attempt to pull a given load the farthest distance.

24. Did the tractor dealers also sell trucks?

For many years, certain IH dealers held franchises for both farm equipment and trucks.

25. Did IH have operations and sales outside the U.S.?

Manufacturing and sales by subsidiaries outside the U.S. were part of IHC since the latter part of the 1800's. Factory locations changed throughout the company history but major plants included Great Britain, France, Germany, Australia, New Zealand, Sweden, Mexico and others at various times. Factory locations changed many times throughout the years. The heaviest concentration was in Europe.

26. Who are the major competitors of International?

Deere would be the largest competitor of CaseIH. Navistar competitors are much more numerous. Some of the major ones would be Kenworth, Peterbilt and Volvo.

27. Were IH tractors imported into the U.S.?

Through the years many IH foreign-built tractors have been brought to the U.S. for sale. The English-built B-414 for instance was sold throughout the U.S. when its features and price better fit the marketplace.

28. Why are the tire treads different on some of the tractors?

The job being performed by a tractor dictates the tread required. For example, a lawn tractor has very smooth tread to avoid tearing up a lawn. A farm tractor pulling a planter needs only a small tread depth for enough traction to pull the planter but not tear up the seedbed. A large tractor pulling a heavy implement such as a disk or plow needs a very aggressive, deep tread to get sufficient traction.

29. Why is the Axial-Flow combine so efficient?

Threshing and separating are performed by a rotor as opposed to the drum and straw walker type models used previously. Great capacity is achieved with the rotor.

30. Is the Axial-Flow combine still offered by Case/IH?

Yes.

31. How many tractors did IH manufacture since it was formed in 1902?

We cannot locate statistics regarding the total number. The number of just one model, the Farmall H reached 391,730. The sale of that model was the largest

154 | IH | SUCCESSES AND FIRSTS

CHAPTER EIGHTEEN

TWO FARM BOYS, RED TRACTORS AND A LEGENDARY PARTNERSHIP

During one of Paul Harvey's daily news and commentary reports that aired on 1,200 radio stations and were heard by 24 million people each week, he said of Orion Samuelson: "He is the voice of the American Farmer."

In 1939, when five-year-old Orion watched with excitement as the implement dealer pulled into the barnyard, he had his sights set a good deal lower. He expected that when he grew up, he would work with his dad on their southwest Wisconsin dairy farm and take over someday when his dad retired. And there had not been a more exciting moment as he watched the unloading of the shiny new Farmall F-20. Its 20-horsepower engine and four-speed transmission made Sid Samuelson's farm chores measurably easier. And, as Paul Harvey reported on his radio program:

> "Orion was eight before his legs were long enough and strong enough to operate the clutch, but that day he became his father's partner, plowing and disking, planting, hay cutting, oats harvesting. Years later, when the farm was sold, the old tractor went with everything else, but 10 years ago the remains were discovered rusting away in a pasture..."

There is a "rest of the story" coming, but first a bit more about how Orion's journey to taking over the family farm veered off course. At age 16, this Wisconsin farm boy fell victim to a rare condition known as Legg-Perthes disease. Surgery was the only way to keep him from being permanently disabled. He spent parts of the next two years in a body cast, recovering in bed, in wheel chairs and on crutches.

While confined to bed, he listened to his favorite radio program, *National Barn Dance* on WLS, a 50,000-watt Chicago radio station, as well as other entertainment and news programs. Faced with a future that did not allow for the rigors of farming, he began to wonder if maybe he could be one of those voices someday. When he finally got back to school, his vocational agriculture teacher encouraged him to enter the FFA's public speaking contests, at which he excelled. And when it was time for college, he convinced his parents to allow him to first attend a broadcasting school in Minneapolis, which led to him landing a job at WKLJ-AM in Sparta, Wisconsin. It was close enough to home that he could still help his dad milk the cows and drive to the radio in time for his shift. That job led to others in Wisconsin, and eventually to WGN Radio and TV in Chicago, where he started work in September of 1960. December 31, 2020, Orion retired with an unprecedented 60 continuous years on the air, using that FFA training to speak at farm breakfasts, county fairs, state fairs and wherever farm groups invited him. Indeed, as Mr. Harvey stated, Orion was "the voice of the American farmer."

Now, the rest of the story about that F-20.

After Sid retired and had his farm auction, the F-20 wound up at a neighbor's farm where it was used until it could be used no more. As happens to most obsolete farm equipment, it was retired to an out-of-the-way part of a pasture where it was left to rust and serve as a rubbing post for cows.

Enter Max Armstrong — but first a little of his back story. Around the same time Orion joined WGN in 1960, a seven-year-old farm boy near Owensville, Indiana, was just learning to drive his dad's Farmall Super H. Max loved the farm. He became his dad's shadow in the field. The family often listened to a Chicago radio station 300 miles away: WGN.

Young Max was fascinated by the voices he heard and when he was 11, Allied Radio in Chicago sold a kit for students to build their own radio transmitter. Max assembled it, ran a 30-foot antenna to the chicken coop, and WMAX-AM was born. That was about as far as the signal of the little transmitter went, but at least the chickens heard it.

Helping his dad farm after school and on weekends was job one for Max, but the radio bug had bitten, and Max was hooked. Fast forward through many summers of tilling the fields along the Wabash River on those red tractors, and radio jobs in the heartland of Illinois, and 24-year-old Max found himself being invited to join one of his idols, Orion Samuelson, at WGN Radio. It was a partnership that would last 44 years.

From 1977 till 2009 they shared radio time on WGN, listened to by

Photo from WGN Radio

agricultural people everywhere the WGN signal travelled. In Max's book *Stories From the Heartland,* he wrote, "There has been no better friend to the American farmer than Orion. His grasp of the ag issues and his eagerness to support producers is unrivaled ... but long before social media and the internet, Orion and I were telling agriculture's story on radio, television and at public events."

And through all those years, they were never far from their common bond: red tractors. As Paul Harvey continued his feature on Orion and the F-20, he noted that bond:

> *"Farm broadcaster Max Armstrong had always encouraged Orion to join in his hobby of tractor restoration and what do you know, that Farmall F-20, which was bought new for $720 in 1939 was sold used when the farm was sold in 1965 for $750. And now, the rusty remains have been sold to a*

collector of antique tractors for $6,700, and restored, it will likely bring four times that. And when the old engine comes back to life, just the sound, to a homesick farm boy, just the sound, will be beyond any price."

For this book, Max adds this memory: *"I found out about the old rusty remains from Orion's sister, Norma, who sent me this picture.*

Then I sent Larry Eipers and his nephew Ben up to get it out of the pasture, which belonged to the late Pete Peterson, Orion's cousin. Pete charged me $200 for the privilege of owning the old rusty carcass, which I still think was money well spent. Once it arrived in central Illinois, it was auctioned off and the late Darius Harms ran the bid up on behalf of the International Harvester Collector's Club Chapter 10 in central Illinois to $6,700. The money was donated to the Illinois Ag In The Classroom program to help teachers educate on how food is produced and how we get it. The IH club fixed it up better than new, and it was quite an emotional moment for Orion when he saw it and sat on it for the first time in over 50 years, with his family at his side. The old F-20 makes frequent appearances at fairs and tractor shows in the heartland."

Photo from Orion Samuelson

Max, well known for his enthusiasm for antique equipment, is a collector, too. "Tractor Boy," as he's known to many, bought the family's Farmall Super H when his dad retired from farming, and later purchased his dad's 560. Max's dad also farmed with a Super M, but Max wasn't able to acquire that specific tractor, but he bought a Super M that was then restored by IHCC Chapter Two in Illinois. On the following page are before and after photos of the Armstrong family's 560.

Tractor enthusiasts of all colors enjoy "Max's Tractor Shed," a regular feature on *This Week in AgriBusiness*, the weekly television show Max and Orion co-host on RFD-TV and on over a hundred TV stations nationwide.

Authors Note: On November 8, 2003, Orion was inducted into the National Radio Hall of Fame, introduced by Paul Harvey. Prior to dinner, I stood by the bar and Mr. Harvey joined me briefly. I said, "We share a friend in Orion." He answered in that distinctive baritone that came through the radio speaker, "Aren't we lucky!"

SUCCESSES AND FIRSTS

Photos by Max Armstrong

CHAPTER NINETEEN

INTERNATIONAL HARVESTER COLLECTORS CLUB

For a company that went out of business in 1985, the International Harvester brand sure is thriving and dynamic. The brand lives on through active and avid collectors of IH products, most of whom are members of the IH Collectors Club. Organized in July 1990, there are over 7,000 members in 40 active chapters located in 49 states and several other countries.

The club promotes the collecting, restoration and showing of IH products, culminating with the annual Red Power Roundup. The restorations, in many cases, are breathtaking, taking aging farmers back to the days decades ago when the shiny, new equipment was delivered to the barnyard by the dealer.

The author is indebted to Bob Buxton and others at the IHCC for their invaluable assistance in the creation of this book.

Photo by Max Armstrong
Two examples of the attention to detail used in the restoration process.

National International Harvester Collectors Club, Inc.

Officers

President
Robert Buxton (2021)
7999 Hwy. HH
Catawissa, MO 63015
(636) 234-4982
rbuxton1943@gmail.com

Vice President
Joe Neville (2019)
1201 W State Street
Williamsburg, IA 52361
319-668-9424
bandjoe@mchsi.com

Secretary
Gary Spina (2020)
6205 Highview Dr. SE
Cedar Rapids, IA 52403
319- 366-3019
spinaih106@gmail.com

Treasurer
Doug Hrbek (2022)
220 E. Grant St.
West Point, NE 68788-1817
402-380-1482
DHrbek@cableone.net

Membership Information:
IH Collectors-Membership Dept.
c/o Lisa Merkle
P.O. Box 179
Middle Point, OH 45863
419-230-0250
IHCCMembership@hotmail.com

Directors

Neil Fishel (2021)
1522 Jasper Lane
Winston-Salem, NC 27127
(336) 408-3324
nfpkyford@yahoo.com

Sherman Roberts (2021)
10766 Hwy 78
Jasper, AL 35501
shermanihc@yahoo.com

Andrew Dawson (2022)
30164 Nashville Ave.
Macon, MO 63552-4219
660-346-0319
ihctractors@yahoo.com

Doug Etzkorn (2023)
18221 CR 25A
Wapakoneta, OH 45895
(419) 234-2486
dncetz@bright.net

Jerome Ripperda (2023)
9303 Pioneer Road
Bartelso, IL 62218
618-381-5614
jbripperda@gmail.com

National International Harvester Collectors Club, Inc.

#1 Missouri
30164 Nashville Avenue
Macon, MO 63552-4219
660-346-0319
Andrew Dawson

#2 Northern Illinois
P.O. Box 445
3783 Minkler Road
Oswego, IL 60543
630-816-0604
Ken Wolf

#3 Kansas
2300 E. Timber Creek
Derby, KS 67034
316-789-9825
Ron Schmitt

#4 Wisconsin
N2661 County Road C
Darien, WI 53114
262-949-0552
Gene Williams

#5 Iowa
1777 Hunter Ave.
Newton, IA 50208
641-521-0029
Jeff Eldred

#6 Ohio
4900 E Twp Road 122
Republic, Ohio 44867
419-618--0017
Steve Smith

#7 Indiana
7345 N County Road 250W
Osgood, IN 47037
812-852-2660
Dawn Dieckmann

#8 Southeastern Pennsylvania
7 Mill Race Road
Wilmington, DE 19810
302-593-8525
Steven Lewis

#9 Tennessee
220 Briscoe Road
Blaine, TN 37709-5610
865-696-0700
Josh Roach

#10 Central Illinois
2217 CR 2200 E
St. Joseph, IL 61873
217-694-4192
J.C. Reitmeier

#11 Michigan
1888 135th Ave
Hopkins, MI 49328
616-262-5135
Randy Marklevitz

#12 Nebraska
P.O. Box 212
Curtis, NE 69025
308-650-1527
Howard Raymond

#14 California
113 Econome Court
Folsom CA 95630
916-983-6415
Roger Lubiens

#15 Minnesota
308 5th St. NW
Montgomery, MN 56069
612-708-9820
William (Bill) M. Ridail

#16 Western Pennsylvania
134 Cole Road
Sandy Lake, PA 16145
724-376-4047
Tom Sharp

National International Harvester Collectors Club, Inc.

#17 Central Pennsylvania
123 Cypress Lane
Lewisburg PA 17837
570-522-7038 (Evenings)
Ben Trapani

#18 New England
30 Lincoln Street
Stoneham, MA 02180-2502
508-523-6835
Mark Wells

#20 Ontario Canada
16 Atchison Lane
Fergus, Ontario
N1M 3K1 Canada
519-577-1615
Kris Switzer

#21 South Dakota
39350 179th St.
Redfield, SD 57469-9438
605-460-0197
Steve Masat

#22 Sweden
Hyllstofta 6622
26493 Klippan Sweden
01146 730 836331
(+7 hours from US CT)
Jan Arvidsson

#23 Alabama
1798 Lauren Lane
Auburn, AL 36830
334-319-4951
Randy Bodine

#24 Kentucky
P.O. Box 1874
Russell Springs, KY 42642
270-585-3227
Glen Whitis

#25 Texas
Lone Star IHCC
10471 County Road 466
Princeton, TX 75407-2276
214-449-0903
James Smith

#26 Minn-Dak
12930 37th Street
Clear Lake, MN 55319
320-743-2889
Jim Becker

#27 Florida
4800 Tiger Lane
Mims, FL 32754
321-268-5072
Charles G. Stevenson

#29 Georgia
100 Sharon Pkwy
Griffin, GA 30224-7457
404-277-1646
Terry Pearce

#31 Louisiana
29846 Hwy 441
Holden, La. 70744
225-567-5539
Tim Hill

#32 Southern Illinois
291 Post Oak Rd
Campbell Hill, IL 62916
618-318-9358
Paul Olson

#33 Northern Indiana
5262 W. 475 N.
Rochester, IN 46975-7724
574-727-1143
Carl Overmyer

#35 New York
1036 Long Pond Rd.
Rochester, NY 14626
585-225-7218
Gene Preston

National International Harvester Collectors Club, Inc.

#36 N E Pennsylvania
464 Duck Harbor Road
Equinunk, Pa. 18417-3033
570-224-4200
Allen E. Johannes

#37 Eastern North Carolina
1708 Broadway Road
Sanford, NC 27332
919-770-0789
Chuck Mann

#38 Western Canada
Apt. 804 2720 College Ave.
Regina, Saskatchewan S4T 1T9
306-541-5800
Iain Richardson

#39 Maryland
12506 Woodsboro Pike
Keymar, MD 21757
240-440-4403
Joseph Speak

#40 Montana
4353 Arnold Road
Shepherd, MT 59079
406-690-5087
Richard Gee

#41 Virginia
761 Harmony Orchard Road
Front Royal, VA 22630
540-660-2403
David Rushton

#42 North Carolina
6225 Reidsville Rd.
Kernersville, NC 27284
336-408-3324
Neil Fishel

#43 Appalachian Mountain
Region of North Carolina
117 Morgan Road
Hendersonville, NC 28793
828-674-4205
Les McCarson

#44 Mississippi
317 New Hope Trail NE
Brookhaven, MS 39601-8071
601-754-5100
Guy H. Nix III

#45 Great Britain
14 Moor Road
Collingham, Newark,
Nottinghamshire, DN22 8DW
UK
828-044-1636-893-066
Michael Hart

IH Museums, Historical Places, and Collections

★ 1. Ron & Jan Wallace
560 N. Goetze Rd.
Carsonville, MI 48419
810-657-9786
ron.ihcollector@airadv.net

★ 2. Changing Seasons/
Growing of America
Mid West Old Threshers
Mt. Pleasant, IA
319-385-8937

★ 3. McCormick's Farm
I-81 Exit 205
Central Virginia
540-377-2255

★ 4. National Automotive and
Truck Museum of the
United States (NATMUS)
1000 Gordon M Buehrig Place
Auburn, IN 46706
260-925-9100
www.natmus.org

★ 5. Rush IH Antique Farm Display
Dale & Norma Rush
Griswold, IA 51535
712-778-2213

★ 6. Wisconsin Historical
Society Stonefield Village
and Wisconsin State
Agricultural Museum
1 mile north of Cassville
Wisconsin on County Hwy. VV
608-725-5210
www.wisconsinhistory.org/stonefield/

★ 7. David Saville
Box 460
Rosetown SK SOL 2V0
306-882-3938 • 306-831-7518 (c)
savid@sasktel.net

★ 8. John & Barb Wagner
69515 Crooked Creek Rd.
White Pigeon, MI 49099
269-483-9093

★ 9. Dan Agee
17593 E. Tally Bend Rd.
Nevada, MO 64772
417-944-2085

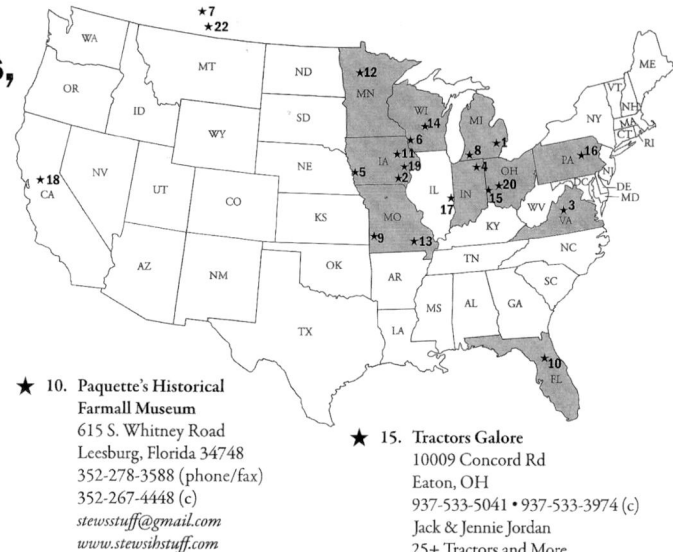

★ 10. Paquette's Historical
Farmall Museum
615 S. Whitney Road
Leesburg, Florida 34748
352-278-3588 (phone/fax)
352-267-4448 (c)
stewsstuff@gmail.com
www.stewsihstuff.com

★ 11. Marv & Bonnie Rohlena
IH/Farmall Collection
Featuring Wheatland Tractors
6637 15th Ave.
Keystone, IA 52249
319-442-3592
mrohlena@netins.net

★ 12. Kevin Happke
Rolling Hills Greenhouse
Implement & Museum
321 Main Street North
Pierz, MN 56364
320-468-6474
321main@gmail.com

★ 13. Laseter Farms -
IH/Farmall Collection
85 Laseter Drive
Sikeston, MO 63801
573-471-5949 • 573-380-4040 (c)
laseterfarms@hotmail.com

★ 14. Huber Brothers
3848 City Rd P
Oxford, WI 53952
608-586-5485 • 608-697-7653 (c)
Located 12 miles off I90-94
at Wisconsin Dells.

★ 15. Tractors Galore
10009 Concord Rd
Eaton, OH
937-533-5041 • 937-533-3974 (c)
Jack & Jennie Jordan
25+ Tractors and More

★ 16. Chapter 17 IH
Proto-type Building
Millville, PA 17846
570-522-7038 • 570-971-3232
Open By Appointment

★ 17. Forsythe Family Farms
IL Route 1 and E2150 Rd.
Marshall, IL 62441
217-826-3100 • 217-826-3865 (f)

★ 18. California Ag Museum
1962 Hays Lane
Woodland, CA 95776
530-666-7700
www.californiaagmuseum.org

★ 19. Red Power Museum
Roger and Bev Howe
Columbus Jct., Iowa 52738
319-321-1818
Visitors always welcome
redpowermuseum@gmail.com

★ 20. Scout Truck & Tractor Museum
Scout/Light Line Distributors
Super Scout Specialist, Inc.
Complex
6711 Dayton Springfield Rd
Enon, Ohio 45323

★ 21. Sukanen Ship Pioneer Village
and Museum
SK-2, Moose Jaw No. 161,
SK S6H 7T2, Canada
306-693-7315

International Harvester Collectors Inc.

Join your friends in collecting, preserving, and displaying the varied products of the International Harvester Company

Membership includes the quarterly publication *Harvester Highlights* with free ad, Red Power Round Up and Winter Convention participation, as well as limited liability insurance at club-sanctioned events.

For membership information, contact:
IHCC Membership
PO Box 179
Middle Point, OH 45863
Phone: 419-230-0250
Email: IHCCMembership@hotmail.com

For more information, visit our website:
www.nationalihcollectors.com

CornBinder Connection

The magazine published quarterly for IH Truck & Scout fans everywhere!

Since 2012

We are a full color publication exclusively covering all International Harvester Trucks & Scouts. All back issues are still available. To find out more information about our magazine, log onto our website at: www.cornbinderconnection.com or write to us at the address below:

Cornbinder Connection, P.O. Box 1827, Butler, PA 16003
email: Sell@cornbinderconnection.com
Phone: **(724) 355-5662**

Cadet Connection Magazine

Published quarterly for Cub Cadet owners, collectors & enthusiasts!

Since 2001

Covering the Cub Cadet line of Power Equipment from 1961 to present. Also covering Cub and Cub Lo-Boys.

To find out more information about our magazine, log onto our website at: www.cadetconnection.com or write to us at the address below:

Cadet Connection, P.O. Box 1827, Butler, PA 16003
email: Sell@cadetconnection.com
Phone: **(724) 355-5662**

HOME OF THE MUSCLE TRACTOR
FOCUSING ON 1960–1990 FARM EQUIPMENT

HERITAGE IRON magazine

The leading source of information on all your favorite tractors and equipment from the muscle era!

6 issues per year Only $29 a year in the U.S.A.

VISA • MasterCard • Discover

- Tractor & Machinery Specs
- Informative Brand History
- Upcoming Events & Classifieds
- Full-Color Magazine

3-POINT INK
PO Box 519
Greenville, IL 62246

HERITAGEIRON.com
855-OLD-IRON

RED POWER magazine

Red Power Magazine Features International Harvester

- IH Tractors • Collectibles
- Hard-to-Find Parts • Farm Equipment
- IH History • Trucks • Cub Cadet • IH Toys

SUBSCRIBE TODAY!

$29.50 per year Bi-Monthly
(Iowa Residents need to add 6% sales tax)
Foreign Subscriptions also available

Call: 712-364-2131
Or find our order form online at
www.redpowermagazine.com

VISA • DISCOVER NETWORK • MasterCard

Red Power Magazine • P.O. Box 245, Ida Grove, IA 51445-0245

ACKNOWLEDGMENTS

So many friends, retired dealers and Harvester people provided valuable information, support and encouragement, and I am grateful to all.

Specifically, IHCC President Bob Buxton (page 161) and good friend Max Armstrong got me started. A very special thanks goes to Navistar Historian Tom Clark. He provided rare, historic photos from Navistar and arranged photo clearance. With his help, we had access to the phenomenal IH archives at Wisconsin Historical Society. Its collection of rarely seen Harvester photos added immeasurably to this book.

Retired IH executives Dale Simpson (page 116) and Jay Suchland (page 139) provided rare insights into major domestic and foreign programs. Hal Beitlich (page 46) and Jeff Wallem (page 78) shared experiences with IH products that will bring back memories for a lot of us. Brian Sells of *Cadet Connections Magazine* and collector Paul Tombaugh provided much-needed background on Cub Cadet history. Retired IH engineer and Cub Cadet designer Keith Burnham and his son Jim (page 70) provided rare drawings and details about the Cadet design. Mike Silberhorn is retired from IH and Cub Cadet Corporation, and provided more details as well as a lot of help in other areas of this book, including the Axial-Flow chapter (page 52). Ryan Duvall of *HarvesterHomecoming.com* (page 52) wrote about the secret Axial-Flow program at the Ft. Wayne Truck Plant, and ex-Moline Works supervisor Tom Taylor (page 56) and ex-dealer Roy Hummel (page 56) added their Axial-Flow memories. Our research reached "across the pond" to find UK IH collectors Ron Knight and son Brian (page 59). Dean Bassett (page 116) provided a dealer's perspective on the XL program. IH truck veteran Ron Hahn (pages 25, 29) added to the DT466 engine and IH trucks discussion. Reginald Schroeder (page 20) provided insight into the little-known IH Great Lakes shipping business. And much appreciation to Paquette's Museum (page 148).

Sherry Schaefer (Publisher, *Heritage Iron Magazine*) did a great job marketing my earlier IH book *The Breakup*, and will be doing it again with this book.

This is the fourth time I get to express gratitude to editors Diane Montiel and Steve Alexander of Bantry Bay Publishing. They somehow gather together all the pieces I send to them and make a book from it all. They continue to amaze me with their skill and artwork.

Finally, I am grateful to my wife Joan for her constant support, recollections of events in my IH past that I had long forgotten, and her proofreading skills. Badly needed computer help was constantly available from our son Steve. Even while filming during a TV episode he would answer my calls for laptop help. Many others helped in many ways to tell this story about "When Red was King." I thank you all.

Paul Wallem

Other books *by* Paul Wallem

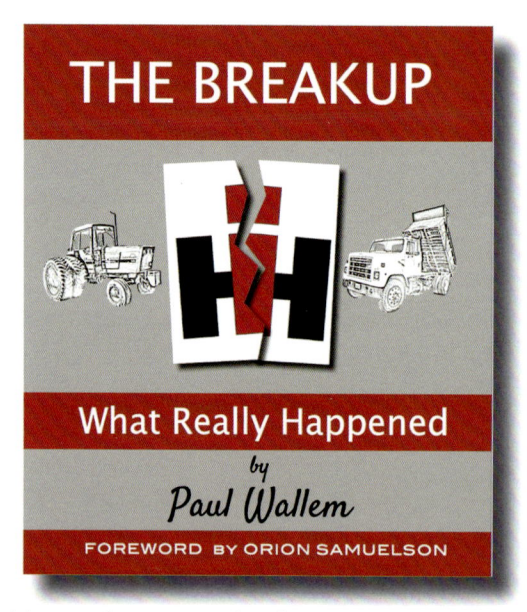

To purchase, email info@3PointInk.com

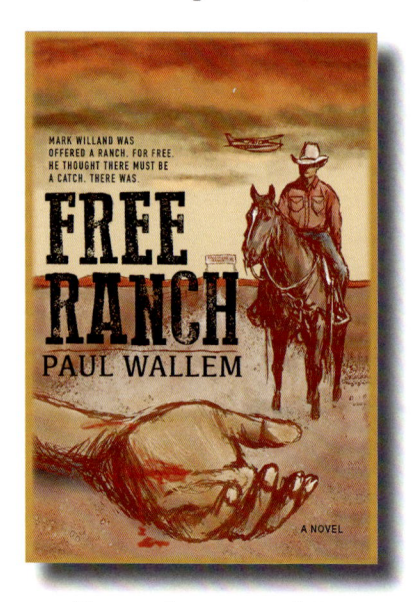

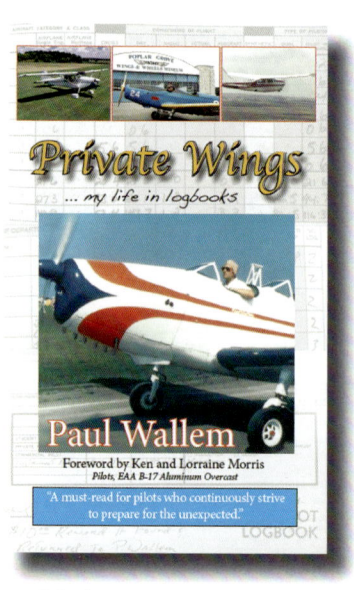

To purchase, email BantryBayPublishing@gmail.com